A
Pocket
Guide
to the
BIG
ISLAND

text by **Curt Sanburn**
photography by **Douglas Peebles**

MUTUAL PUBLISHING

Library of Congress Catalog Card
Number: 00-100556

First Printing, August 2000
1 2 3 4 5 6 7 8 9

Design by Jane Hopkins

ISBN 1-56647-160-5

Mutual Publishing
1215 Center Street, Suite 210
Honolulu, Hawaii 96816
Telephone (808) 732-1709
Fax (808) 734-4094
e-mail: mutual@lava.net
www.mutualpublishing.com

Printed in Thailand

TABLE OF CONTENTS

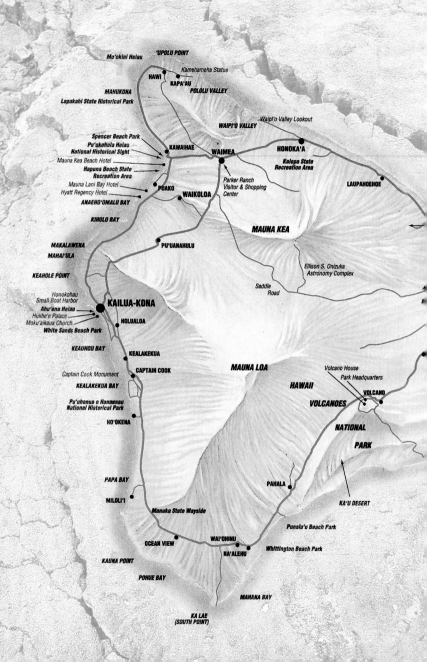

BIG ISLAND
FACTS & FIGURES

County: Hawai'i
County seat: Hilo
Land area: 4,028.2 square miles
Resident population: 142,390 (1999)
Highest point: Mauna Kea summit, 13,796 feet
Shoreline: 266 miles
Extreme length and width: 93 miles by 76 miles
Average annual temperature: Hilo: 72.2°F (1999)
Highest recorded temperature: 100°F
Lowest recorded temperature (at sea level): 52°F;
    at Mauna Kea's summit: 1.4°F
Average annual rainfall, at Kawaihae: 10 inches;
    Hilo Airport: 128 inches
Chief industries: tourism, agriculture, construction
Energy sources: 95% from imported oil
Hotel and condominium rental units: 9,655 (1998)
Visitors per year: 1,259,860 (1999)
Average number of visitors per day: 23,120 (1998)
Public and private golf courses: 17
Public tennis courts: 45
National Parks: 4
State Parks: 16
County Parks: 135

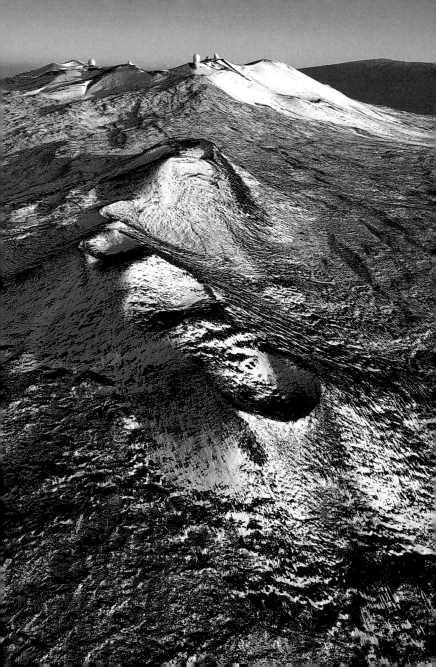

INTRODUCTION

THE ISLAND OF HAWAI'I or, as it is commonly called by locals, the Big Island, has only a thin layer of man-made environs spread across miles of lava, scrub, and forest. That's because nature looms large on this island, and nothing else really compares.

The island's two major shield volcanoes, Mauna Kea and Mauna Loa, climb almost 14,000 feet above the Pacific. Their wide slopes join the peaks of three smaller volcanoes on the island's

THE ANCIENT HAWAIIAN PEOPLE THRIVED BECAUSE OF THEIR CLOSE CONNECTION TO THE NATURAL FORCES OF THE LAND. *HULA*, THE DANCE OF THIS CULTURE, MIMICS IN HUMAN GESTURE AND MOTION THE CHARACTERISTCS ASSOCIATED WITH THESE ELEMENTAL FORCES.

＊　　　＊　　　＊　　　＊　　　＊

irregular perimeter: Kohala, Hualālai, and Kīlauea (the active one). In combination, these broad mountains create the land and shore of the Big Island. Northeast trade winds stream across the smooth, young landscape, dropping their moisture on the high windward rain forests, funneling through the saddle areas, accelerating down the gentle, leeward declines, and eddying around Mauna Loa's buxom mass.

Within the last 200 years (Hawai'i's period of recorded history), over one hundred volcanic eruptions have sent lava rivers into various precincts all over the island's southern half. These rivers are part of the nonstop process that began a million years ago and that still builds the island. Towns and beaches are overrun

OPPOSITE PAGE: JUST ABOVE THE CLOUDS ON MAUNA KEA RISES A CLUSTER OF BUILDINGS THAT HOUSE ONE OF THE WORLD'S MOST SOPHISTICATED OBSERVATORY SYSTEMS. IN HAWAIIAN LEGEND, THIS COLD AND BARREN VOLCANIC PEAK WAS HOME TO THE SNOW GODDESS POLI'AHU. ALTHOUGH PELE, THE VOLCANO GODDESS, FROM HER HOME ON MAUNA LOA, HURLED FIERY ROCK AND SPEWED LAVA TOWARD POLI'AHU, THE ICE MAIDEN REMAINED UNTOUCHED IN HER DOMAIN OF WINTRY CLOUDS.

and they vanish. New land appears, new little cinder cones, new beaches. Earthquakes occasionally drop sections of coastline a foot or two. Roads close.

The Big Island is alive. Its growth is measured in decades, not millennia. A dynamic energy animates the whole landscape, whether it's actually bubbling with magma or not. It's hard to describe this living land adequately. It has to be felt.

After a century of ranching, fishing, and agriculture, the island has become an international curiosity: the home of an active, drive-in volcano, and mega-hotels built on lava rocks at the edges of idyllic, jewel-like beaches. Its sleepy little towns have started to fuss about traffic lights. Suddenly it seems that the entire world is driving past the little post office, flashing cameras, and squinting at road maps.

Yet the new grand hotels, airports, roads, shopping centers, and warehouse districts are still dwarfed by all the outdoor grandeur. The overwhelming scale of the island—and the power it suggests—renders everything else insignificant.

The Hawaiians understood this. Remnants of their life as it was before the *haoles* (foreigners; Caucasians) arrived are rather insubstantial: just a

✿ ✿ ✿ ✿

SURF POUNDS THE BLACK LAVA SHORELINE ON THE BIG ISLAND'S RUGGED KONA COAST, AND SPEWS A BILLOWING SHROUD OF SPINDRIFT INTO THE GOLDEN LIGHT OF SUNSET. THIS MAGNIFICENT SCENE, REPEATED EACH DAY, IS PART OF THE RAW BEAUTY AND AWESOME POWER OF THIS YOUNG ISLAND.

few trails, agricultural terraces, fishponds, walls, rock carvings (petroglyphs), shelter sites, and several large platforms of rock, called *heiau*. These stony ramparts were built atop hills or at strategic harbors or on advantageous fields. *Heiau* were places of worship and ritual, dedicated to fishing gods, gods of the fields, the great lizard gods (*mo'o*), war gods, and the ancestral gods of the great chiefs. Men, gods, and nature met at the stone altars to honor the sacred compacts which bound them inextricably and fearfully together. Those who study the history and culture of the Hawaiians invariably note the remarkable harmony with nature sustained by these muscular Polynesians, who used their unsurpassed seafaring arts to find Paradise.

They first landed at South Point, Ka Lae, on the Big Island about 1,500 years ago. Westerners, or what the Hawaiians politely called *haoles*, arrived in 1778, when Captain James Cook of His Majesty's Navy discovered Kaua'i. A year later Cook's ships returned, anchoring at Kealakekua Bay, a few miles south of today's Kailua-Kona. The British captain was royally feted; but later he was clubbed to death in a scuffle, when

THE LARGE *PILI*-GRASS BUILDING AT THE PLACE OF REFUGE IN HONAUNAU IS PART OF A RECONSTRUCTED *HEIAU* KNOWN AS THE HALE O KEAWE (HOUSE OF KEAWE). BUILT BY CHIEF KEAWE TO CONTAIN HIS BONES AND THOSE OF HIS RELATIVES, THIS MAUSOLEUM IS THE ONLY VISIBLE STRUCTURE ALONG THE PROTECTED BAY.

some Hawaiians stole a ship's launch and caused a confrontation. A shooting incident followed. To shield themselves from British bullets, the Hawaiian villagers held up flimsy mats woven from the leaves of the *hala* tree.

One young chief who watched the brief barrage was Kamehameha, the Lonely One, who would later conquer the Big Island, Maui, and O'ahu with the help of *haole* guns. He established the Kamehameha dynasty and the Kingdom of Hawai'i, which lasted over 100 years.

New England missionaries arrived at Kailua-Kona in 1819. Eight short decades later the Hawaiian Islands were annexed by the United States. During the intervening years, the Hawaiian population, ravaged by introduced diseases, declined from at least 300,000 to an estimated 50,000.

By the time of annexation, the lands of Hawai'i had already shifted to private ownership and had been consolidated in huge *haole*-owned cattle ranches and sugar plantations. A small cattle herd left in Kohala by English captain George Vancouver as a gift for the chief Kamehameha became the nucleus for what is now the Parker Ranch and its impressive 225,000 acres of ranch land and 55,000 head of cattle.

THE SPECTACULAR LAVA FOUNTAINS OF
THE PU'U O'O VENT, PART OF THE
KĪLAUEA VOLCANO NETWORK IN THE
BIG ISLAND'S HAWAI'I VOLCANOES
NATIONAL PARK, HAVE ENTERTAINED
SCIENTISTS, PHOTOGRAPHERS, AND
SIGHTSEERS FROM ALL OVER THE WORLD.

The sugar plantation managers of the Hamakua and Ka'u districts, in need of cheap and dependable labor, arranged for the immigration of foreign workers into Hawai'i to tend and harvest the profitable sugar fields. First, laborers came from China, then Portugal, Japan, Korea, Okinawa, and, finally, the Philippines. They did the backbreaking work, fulfilled their contracts, saved money, started families, and eventually moved from the plantation camps into towns or to O'ahu.

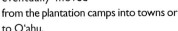

THE LOOMING FIGURES OF *KI'I*, OR SACRED IMAGES, EMBODIED PAGANISM TO THE FIRST MISSIONARIES.

✳ ✳ ✳

Coffee groves in Kona, lettuce fields in Kamuela, macadamia orchards in Ka'u, and cow pastures in Kohala give the Big Island relief from the endless plantation "lawns" that characterize the other islands. Diversified agriculture has allowed each of the island's far-flung rural communities to develop its own unique character.

Hilo, the Big Island's big town, had the airport, seaport, and easy access to Kīlauea volcano, which had been set aside by the U.S. government in 1916 as Hawai'i Volcanoes National Park. Hilo was the logical place for an infant sightseeing industry, and a few hotels were built there in the early 1960s. But the rainy climate kept the visitor counts low, while O'ahu and Maui's visitor industries boomed.

The old royal playground at Kona, 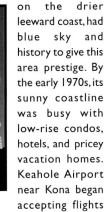 on the drier leeward coast, had blue sky and history to give this area prestige. By the early 1970s, its sunny coastline was busy with low-rise condos, hotels, and pricey vacation homes. Keahole Airport near Kona began accepting flights directly from the mainland.

The big ranches sold huge oceanfront lava fields in South Kohala and North Kona to developers from the mainland and Japan, whose ambitions and financial resources were bigger than anything Hawai'i had ever seen. The resort boom was on.

One landowner who didn't have to sell was the Bishop Estate, the fee-holder to hundreds of thousands of acres on Hawai'i, Maui, and O'ahu. Hawai'i's largest private landholder, Bishop Estate is the legacy of the Kamehameha dynasty, held in perpetual trust for the education and general benefit of Hawaiian children. It has developed a multi-hotel golf resort at Keauhou on lands where the warrior-King Kamehameha I once lived.

It is not certain when Kamehameha was born, because dates had a different meaning to Hawaiian oral historians. Scholars assume it was in the 1750s, in Kohala at ‘Upolu Point, where the supposed birthing site has been sensitively preserved.

As a boy, Kamehameha learned modern warfare and modern commerce and took advantage of both. He forged the Hawaiian nation from a group of warring chiefdoms and made it prosperous according to the European definition of prosperity. When he died in Kona in 1819 at his compound at Kailua Bay, where the King Kamehameha Hotel now stands, he was an old man still praying to his gods.

The life and legend of Kamehameha pervade the Big Island even today. The touchstones of the island's history and lore are his birthplace at ‘Upolu Point, his great war hei*au* at Pu‘ukohola, his lands at Keauhou, the fishponds at ‘Anaeho‘omalu, his refuge at Waipi‘o, and the site of his death on the shores of Kailua Bay. After his passing, Kamehameha's sacred bones, thought to be the vessels for his immortal spirit, were carried away to a secret burial cave. Although many fortune hunters have searched for this greatest tomb of Hawai‘i's royalty, the cave has never been found.

 ✳   ✳   ✳   ✳

THE PLACE OF REFUGE (*PU‘UOHUNA*) IN THE NORTH KONA DISTRICT WAS ONE OF THE MOST SACRED AREAS ON THE ISLAND OF HAWAI‘I. WITHIN ITS ROCK BOUNDARIES, VIOLATORS OF THE *KAPU* LAWS SOUGHT SANCTUARY AND PURIFICATION, AND WOMEN, CHILDREN, THE ELDERLY, AND THE WEAK FOUND PROTECTION DURING WARS.

A GRASS HUT ON THE GROUNDS OF THE MO'OKINI HEIAU IN NORTH KOHALA WOULD HAVE BEEN CONSIDERED A TYPICAL MEDIUM-SIZED *HALE* IN OLD HAWAI'I. SUCH STRUCTURES ARE RARE TODAY. THIS ONE HOUSED THE *KAHU* (KEEPER OR CARETAKER) OF THE *HEIAU*.

VIGNETTES

An Early Appreciation of Hawaiian Hospitality

"About seven in the evening we reached Halaua, the residence of Miomioi, a friend and favorite of the late king Kamehameha. He gave us a hearty welcome, with the accustomed courtesy of a Hawaiian chief, saying, 'Our house is large and there are plenty of sleeping mats for us.'

"The hospitality of the chiefs . . . is always accompanied with a courtesy of behavior peculiarly gratifying to those who are their guests, and indicating a degree of refinement seldom witnessed among uncivilized nations.

"The usual salutation is Aroha (attachment), or Aroha nui (attachment great); and the customary invitation to partake of some refreshment is, 'The food belonging to you and us is ready; let us eat together'; always using the pronoun *kakou*, or *kaua*, which includes the person addressed, as well as the speaker.

"On entering a chief's house, should we remark, 'Yours is a strong or convenient house,' he would answer, 'It is a good house for you and me.'

"If, on entering a house, or examining a fine canoe or piece of cloth, we should ask who it belongs to, another person would tell us the possessor's name; but if we happened to inquire of the owner himself, he would invariably answer, 'It is yours and mine.' The same desire to please is manifested in a variety of ways."

from The Journal of William Ellis

Ellis, a 28-year-old English missionary and veteran of seven years' work in the Society Islands, traveled around the island of Hawai'i in 1823 with a guide named Makoa. The young Christian was less concerned with the salvation of naked heathens than he was fascinated by the minutiae of a foreign culture. His *Journal* is a sympathetic and insightful firsthand report on Hawai'i as home to a largely intact Polynesian society.

HALEMA'UMA'U CRATER, ONE OF THE MOST IMPRESSIVE OF A CHAIN OF CRATERS ON THE KĪLAUEA VOLCANO, IS 1,300 FEET DEEP AND TEN MILES IN CIRCUMFERENCE. AT FIRST LOOK THE PIT SEEMS DORMANT, BUT THE STEAM VENTS REMIND THE VIEWER OF THE FIERY MOLTEN ROCK RUNNING JUST BELOW THE CRUSTED SURFACE.

✳   ✳   ✳

The Art of Sarcasm as Practiced by Mark Twain, Circa 1873

"Now, let us annex the islands ....We could make sugar enough to supply all America, perhaps, and the prices would be very easy with the duties removed ....And then we could own the mightiest volcano on earth—Kilauea! Barnum could run it—he understands fires now. Let us annex by all means.

"We must annex those people. We can afflict them with our wise and beneficent governments. We can introduce the novelty of thieves, all the way from street-car pickpockets to municipal robbers and government defaulters, and show them how amusing it is to arrest them and try them and then turn them loose—some for cash and some for 'political influence.' We can make them ashamed of their simple and primitive justice ....We can give them juries composed entirely of the most simple and charming leatherheads. We can give them railway corporations who will buy their legislature like old clothes, and run over their best citizens and complain of the corpses for smearing their unpleasant juices on the track. We can ...furnish them some Jay Goulds who will do away with their old-time notion that stealing is not respectable ....We can give them lecturers! I will go myself.

"We can make that little bunch of sleepy islands the hottest corner on earth, and array it in the moral splendor of our high and holy civilization. Annexation is what the poor islanders need. 'Shall we to men benighted, the lamp of life deny?'"

—Mark Twain. A frequent visitor to the islands, Twain added his two cents to the national debate regarding the annexation of Hawai'i to the U.S. in an essay published in 1873. Annexation did not occur until 1900.

Pele of the Sacred Earth
(Pele-Honua-Mea)

Halema'uma'u crater at Kīlauea's sunken summit is the home of Pele, the fire goddess, and her fractious family of lesser fire gods—brothers and sisters with names like Ka-moho-ali'i, the king of steam; Kane-hekili, the husband of thunder; Keo-'ahi-kama-kaua, the fire-thrusting child of war; Hi'iaka-kapu'ena'ena, the red-hot mountain holding clouds. This group of gods is among the most dreadful and fearsome in the Hawaiian pantheon. Pele, especially, is known for her petty jealousies and swift retributions. Rock formations all over Hawai'i are attributed to unfortunates who crossed Pele or flirted with one of her lovers and paid for it with instant petrifaction or inundation by lava.

Pele's first home was on Kaua'i. After a traveler from Puna journeyed to Kaua'i and boasted to Pele of the superior beauty of Puna, he returned to Puna and found it overrun with lava.

Near Kapoho during the festival for the god Lono, Pele, disguised as an old village woman, challenged a handsome young chief to a *holua*

TWO PIERCING LAVA-ORANGE EYES BLAZE THROUGH THE VEIL OF SULPHUR STEAM DURING THE MOST RECENT PHASE OF ERUPTIONS ON KĪLAUEA. WHEN THE FIRE GODDESS PELE CRACKS THE BLACK SURFACE AT THE SUMMIT, THE CRATER OF HALEMA'UMA'U HAS BEEN KNOWN TO FILL WITH LAVA AND BECOME A LAKE OF UNDULATING RED OOZE.

(sledding) race, lost the race, then asked the chief, Kahawali, if she could use his sled in a rematch. Thinking she was just a commoner, he said no. Incensed, Pele transformed herself into a river of lava and pursued Kahawali down the *holua* hill. The chief did not pause in his flight until he had reached O'ahu.

In the most popular Pele story, which is the subject of long chants and somber dances even today, the goddess flooded huge areas of Puna and Ka'u with lava, and destroyed her handsome lover Lohi'au when she wrongly suspected him of faithlessness with her sister Hi'iaka, the patroness of the *hula*.

At Halema'uma'u crater, the goddess is often seen in the mist from the fumaroles that dot the area. Her little white dog, wandering alone or in the company of a melancholy woman in a red *holoku* dress, is sighted throughout the summit area. At the edge of the crater, offerings are left for the goddess who, even today, commands respect. After all, no one really wants to argue with Pele, personification of the infinite and unpredictable power of Kīlauea.

*　　　*　　　*　　　*

SITTING ON A MOUND AMIDST TUFTED CLOUDS AND FIELDS OF WIND-HEWN SNOW, THE MAUNA KEA OBSERVATORY IS A BUZZ OF SCIENTIFIC ACTIVITY DAY AND NIGHT AS TECHNICIANS, ENGINEERS, AND ASTRONOMERS STUDY THE MOVEMENT OF THE STARS AND PLANETS.

NATURAL SPECTACLES

MYTHOLOGY NOTWITHSTANDING, THE ISLANDS of Hawai'i were built by volcanic action beginning over 30 million years ago with Kure Atoll at the northwestern end of the archipelago, and continuing today on the Big Island at the southeastern end of the 1,600-mile-long chain. A slow, steady northwestward drift of the earth's upper layer over a "hot spot" in the deeper layers accounts for the island chain's linear shape and the progressive age of the islands.

The major land form is the typical, broadly rounded "shield" volcano, built up from the ocean floor to heights in excess of two miles above sea level by innumerable thin lava flows. Mauna Loa on the Big Island is a classic—and still active—shield volcano, so gentle in its rise that the drama of its 13,600-foot height above sea level (as high as most Rocky Mountain peaks) is difficult to appreciate.

Viewing the eight major islands, it's easy to see the geological evolution from the broad, swelling shapes of young and intact shield volcanoes on the Big Island and Maui to the heavily eroded, jagged topography of Kaua'i, and finally Ni'ihau, the low, almost completely worn-down remains of an even older shield volcano.

Hualālai, Mauna Loa, and Kīlauea, three of the Big Island's five volcanic peaks, have erupted in the past 200 years. Hualālai was last active in 1801. Kīlauea (in Hawai'i Volcanoes National Park), the most active volcano in the world, continues a particularly destructive eruptive phase.

Mauna Kea, at 13,796 feet, is 100 feet taller than Mauna Loa, the most massive of the state's mountains. Mauna Loa's gentle, endless lava slopes make up half the island's land area, having buried the adjacent lower slopes of all the other volcanoes,

OPPOSITE PAGE: SPECTACULAR WATERFALLS FED BY THE UPLAND STREAMS OF KOHALA TUMBLE INTO DEEP, EMERALD-GREEN PLUNGE POOLS. THESE STREAMS PROVIDED IRRIGATION FOR ANCIENT HAWAIIAN *TARO* FARMERS, AND IN MODERN TIMES HAVE WATERED THE SUGAR PLANTATIONS OF THE DISTRICT.

except Kohala. The most recent activity of the "Long Mountain" was in 1984, when a twenty-two-day flow stopped about ten miles above the suburbs of Hilo, the Big Island's major population center.

The effects of rainfall and its resulting stream erosion are most striking on the Big Island's northeastern, windward side. The Hamakua Coast is scored with streams, waterfalls, and gorges draining Mauna Kea's perpetually wet highlands. The deeply-eroded Waipi'o, Waimanu, and Pololu valleys show the relative age of the Kohala volcano, compared with Mauna Kea's younger, much less-eroded slopes. Dry leeward areas such as the vast South Kohala slope of Mauna Kea show relatively little stream erosion.

Most apparent on windward shores is the erosive activity of the trade wind-driven waves. Spectacular sea cliffs have been carved into the ancient lava flows all along the Hamakua coast.

As Kīlauea's volcanic dome inflates and deflates with liquid magma, the surface rock on the mountain's southeastern coastal flank adjusts. Puna and Ka'u beaches subsided up to ten feet after a 7.2 earthquake in 1975. At Halape, just south of Hawai'i Volcanoes National Park, coconut tree stumps stand in a shallow cove, flooded by a sudden drop of the beach.

Sudden seismic jolts also set off local *tsunamis* ("tidal waves") that further damage this battered coast. In 1868 an extremely severe earthquake and *tsunami* wiped out every fishing village from Cape Kumukahi to South Point. Most were never rebuilt.

Dangerous as it is, the Big Island is dynamic and alive, one of the earth's exceptional places.

✳   ✳   ✳   ✳   ✳

POWERFUL AND VINDICTIVE, PELE PERIODICALLY SETS HER VOLCANO ON FIRE, SENDING MOLTEN ROCK SURGING DOWN THE MOUNTAIN TO THE SEA. CASCADING OVER THE BLACK DEVASTATION OF RECENT ERUPTIONS, THESE RIVULETS PLUNGE IN STEAMY LAVA-FALLS INTO THE WAVES BELOW. THE BRILLIANT HEAT OF THE MAGMA RUNNELS CASTS LUMINESCENT REDS AND VIOLETS ON THE PLUMING CLOUDS OF GAS.

The *hapu'u* or tree fern, with its fuzzy, curled fiddle heads and delicately feathered fronds, thrives in the moist ground cover of rain forests on the slopes of Pele's volcano.

THE TIMELESS BEAUTY OF THE BIG ISLAND'S MANY WATERFALLS HAS INSPIRED GENERATIONS OF VISITORS. THE PRESENCE OF WATER IN A LUSH RAINFOREST SETTING PROVIDES STRONG CONTRAST TO ITS OPPOSITE, FIRE AND LAVA.

The sun makes it way across the cloud-mantled
summit crater of 8,271-foot Hualālai Volcano.
Although this docile-looking mound appears to
be long extinct, the U.S. Geological Survey lists
Hualālai as the fourth most dangerous volcano
in the United States. It last erupted in 1808 and,
according to experts who have been charting its
seismic activity, it has the potential for a Mount
St. Helens-type explosion.

PU'UHONUA O HONAUNAU NATIONAL HISTORICAL
PARK, THE SINGLE MOST IMPRESSIVE REMNANT OF
ANCIENT HAWAI'I ON THE BIG ISLAND.

TOURS
KONA

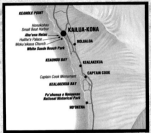

HULIHE'E PALACE, LOCATED ON KAILUA BAY, WAS THE FAVORITE VACATION HOME FOR HAWAI'I'S ROYALTY IN THE NINETEENTH CENTURY.

❊   ❊   ❊   ❊

WHILE KONA'S SUNNY CLIMATE is much praised, the volcanic activity seventy miles away generates volcanic haze, called "vog," that can cloak the area with vapors. The sun shines, but its brilliance may be reduced. The sunsets, however, are other-worldly.

The 1,000-year-old village of Kailua was renamed Kailua-Kona in the 1950s by the U.S. Postal Service to distinguish it from Honolulu's large suburb of Kailua. In a corner of the town's busy bay front is one of Hawai'i's most historic sites: Kamakahonu, the compound where Hawai'i's great King Kamehameha, who was responsible for unifying the Islands, spent his last years and where he died on May 8, 1819. Now a National Historic Landmark within the grounds of the King Kamehameha Hotel, it includes a small white-sand cove and the restored 'Ahuena Heiau, prominent on a lava-rock platform built into the shallow water at the edge of a lagoon. It is said the great warrior king chose this spot to keep an eye on his farms in the highlands above the village.

It was also at Kamakahonu that soon after Kamehameha's death, his favorite wife Ka'ahumanu, impressed by the relative quality of foreign men and women, led the overthrow of the *kapu* system of very strict laws and practices by sitting with male members of the royal family for a meal. Indeed, she ate a banana, hitherto strictly forbidden to women. When nothing happened to her, much of Hawaiian society's belief structure quickly collapsed.

On March 30, 1820, the first New England missionaries stepped ashore at Kamakahonu and received royal permission from Queen Ka'ahumanu and young

King Liholiho to work for one year among the *maka'ainana* (commoners). The timing of their arrival, given the spiritual void that had descended on the islands with the collapse of the *kapu* system, could be called "providential."

Daily guided tours of Kamakahonu, courtesy of the hotel, include explanations of the historical objects and illustrations on display in the hotel lobby.

Blessed with calm, deep offshore waters, the Kona coast is one of the world's great game-fishing locales, with Kailua-Kona its headquarters. Next to Kamakahonu's beach is the busy Kona Pier, where tour and dinner-cruise boats tie up. Daily, at noon and again at about 3:30 p.m., the pier takes on a special buzz as charter fishermen weigh their catches of huge blue, black, and striped marlin up to 1,000 pounds, giant yellowfin tuna, *mahimahi*, and even an occasional shark. Honokohau Harbor, about two miles north of Kona, is the charter game-fishing center.

Kona's history as a royal retreat continued well into the nineteenth century, when John Adams Kuakini, King Kamehameha's brother-in-law, built

TOURISTS LEARN THE TEAM SKILL OF PADDLING OUTRIGGR CANOES IN THE PROTECTIVE LAGOON AT THE MAUNA LANI RESORT IN KAILUA-KONA.

   ✳   ✳   ✳

Hulihe'e Palace across the harbor from Kamakahonu. The palace, circa 1838, was enjoyed best by Hawai'i's "Merrie Monarch," King David Kalakaua, during the 1880s, when he entertained there lavishly and often. The house is now maintained by the Daughters of Hawai'i, who charge a small admission fee to see its cool rooms, Hawaiian artifacts, and opulent royal furniture.

The gated, lava-rock and coral-mortared Moku'aikaua Church is directly across from the Palace on Ali'i Drive. Built in 1836, it is a descendant of Hawai'i's first Christian church, built in 1826 at this same site with stones from a *heiau*. The original sixty-foot-long and thirty-foot-wide Hawaiian thatch building burned down. In the sanctuary of the present-day church, beautiful *koa* and *'ohi'a* wood furnishings reveal its colorful history.

Numerous shopping centers line Ali'i Drive, the town's main street. Very local Oceanview Inn overlooks Ali'i Drive traffic at the spot where the annual Ironman Triathalon finishes. The inn's restaurant, with fifty-year-old traditions and inexpensive ethnic food, is an easy escape from standard tourist fare.

CHARTERED DEEP-SEA FISHING BOATS SET OUT EARLY EVERY MORNING FROM KONA PIER, WITH A STEADY CLIENTELE OF SPORTS FISHERMEN FROM ALL OVER THE WORLD.

A COLORFUL FLEET OF FISHING BOATS AND OUTRIGGER CANOES SHARE A BEACH ON THE LEEWARD COAST OF THE BIG ISLAND. THE CALM WATERS IN THIS AREA ARE ALIVE WITH TROPICAL DEEP-SEA (PELAGIC) FISHES, PROVIDING FISHERMEN WITH A PROFITABLE CATCH.

Kona Inn Shopping Village is on the grounds of the legendary Kona Inn, a sprawling, lodge-style hotel built in 1928. The seaside lawns of the old inn are still intact and particularly lovely at sunset. Famous visitors like Will Rogers, Ernest Hemingway, Barbara Hutton, and Cecil B. de Mille came here to hunt, fish, and hang out.

Ali'i Drive continues south along the rocky shore past private homes, condos, small hotels, the distinctive Royal Kona Resort, and a few beaches, notably White Sand Beach, and Kahalu'u Beach Park. In former times, heavily populated Kahalu'u was a prosperous Hawaiian village. Of interest are the area's archaeological fragments, petroglyphs, and house sites, as well as tiny St. Peter's Catholic Church.

Next along the road is Keauhou; Kamehameha's son and Hawai'i's third king, Kauikeaouli, was born at Keauhou. This area is rich with precontact Hawaiian history and lore. On some of the properties there are historic sites including petroglyphs carved on the rocks which can be seen at low tide, and several heiaus. According to myth, there were human sacrifices at one of the heiau.

Ali'i Drive dead-ends just beyond Keauhou. Backtrack to Kailua-Kona and take Hualālai Road a few miles up the slope to Holualoa, a charming artists' colony and coffee-growing center. At the junction of Hualālai Road and Route 180, turn left. Downtown Holualoa is a collection of ramshackle buildings, including the landmark Kona Hotel, where a room (with shared bath) costs under $30 a night. In the same neighborhood are several fascinating art galleries.

Head south on Route 180 through the rich fields of Kona, where today's big cash crops include Kona coffee, macadamia nuts, and oranges. Several coffee companies offer tours and tastings. Old churches, each one more picturesque than the next, lure both worshippers and photographers.

LOOKING INLAND ACROSS THE WATERS OF ALAHAKA BAY, TO THE CANOE LANDING AND COCONUT GROVE FRONTING THE VISITOR CENTER OF PU'UHONUA O HONAUNAU NATIONAL HISTORICAL PARK, THIS VIEW CAN BE SEEN ONLY FROM A POSITION IN THE MIDDLE OF THE BAY. AN IDEAL SPOT FOR SNORKELING, PICNICKING, OR JUST HANGING OUT, THE SHALLOW WATERS PROVIDE THE PERFECT PLACE TO COOL OFF AFTER THE LONG DRIVE.

✻   ✻   ✻

FAR LEFT: TINY ST. PETER'S CHURCH, ON A PICTURESQUE SEASIDE PLOT OF LAND IN KONA, WAS ONE OF THE FIRST CATHOLIC MISSIONS ON THE ISLAND OF HAWAI'I.

LEFT: WORLD-RENOWNED, AND LOCALLY ADORED, CHEF SAM CHOY IS A PROMINENT FIGURE IN THE KONA AREA. HIS RESTAURANTS OFFER LOCAL-STYLE CUISINE THAT WILL SATISFY THE MOST DISCRIMINATING PALATE.

LEI STANDS AND FLOWER VENDORS LINE THE STREETS IN KAILUA-KONA. THESE EXQUISITE ORCHID BLOSSOMS WERE FIRST BROUGHT TO HAWAI'I BY CHINESE IMMIGRANTS AND, SINCE THEN, HUNDREDS OF SPECIES AND HYBRIDS HAVE BEEN DEVELOPED.

Route 180 intersects Route 11 (Mamalahoa High-way) at Honalo and continues through the growing towns of Kealakekua and Captain Cook. At the latter, a right turn onto Napoʻo-poʻo Road begins a gorgeous descent almost 1,500 feet to historic Kealakekua Bay and the village of Nāpōʻopoʻo.

At the beach, the high walls of Hikiau Heiau mark Nāpōʻopoʻo Beach Park, ideal for snorkeling, scenery, and history. Across the bay, although inaccessible, near

LOCAL CHILDREN COLLECT FRUIT FROM THE TREES IN THEIR YARDS AND PUT THEM ON ROADSIDE TABLES TO SELL, MUCH LIKE MAINLAND CHILDREN SELL LEMONADE ON HOT SUMMER DAYS. MANGOES GROW WILD IN PARTS OF THE KAILUA-KONA COUNTRYSIDE.

✻   ✻   ✻

the abandoned village of Kaʻawaloa, Captain James Cook—whose expedition "discovered" Hawaiʻi—had his tragic encounter with the Hawaiians. Where Cook fell is marked by a white obelisk erected by his countrymen in 1874.

Kealakekua Bay offers some of the island's best snorkeling, so be prepared for crowds. Excursion boats from Kailua-Kona and Keauhou bring snorkeling and diving groups eager to see the fish and the colorful coral.

Four miles south on the narrow coast road out of Napoʻopoʻo, past the fields of Mokuʻohai—where a bloody, eight-day battle established Kamehameha as the ruler of the island in 1782—is Puʻuhonua o Honaunau National Historical Park, the single most impressive remnant of ancient Hawaiʻi on the Big Island. The broad lava point at Honaunau Bay, covered by a large coconut grove and surrounded on three sides by blue water, is barricaded at its *mauka* (mountain) side by a massive stone wall 1,000 feet long, ten feet high, and fifteen feet wide. The land contained within was a *puʻuhonua* (a place of refuge or safe sanctuary) where *kapu* breakers, defeated warriors, and others facing mortal punishment were safe. Many fugitives swam across the bay to reach protection. Once inside, and after the *kahuna pule* (priest) had performed absolving rites, fugitives were free to leave and resume normal life without fear. In ancient Hawaiʻi *puʻuhonua* existed on all the islands. The Big Island had at least six. The innocent and the guilty alike could escape certain death simply by crossing the sacred thresholds.

CAPTAIN COOK WAS TREATED LIKE A HIGH CHIEF WHEN HE SAILED INTO KEALAKEKUA BAY IN 1779. HE AND HIS MEN STAYED IN THE AREA FOR SEVERAL WEEKS COLLECTING PROVISIONS FOR THEIR TWO SHIPS, THEN SAILED NORTH. A STORM HIT THE SHIPS OFF THE COAST OF KOHALA AND SPLIT A MAST, FORCING A RETURN TO KEALAKEKUA. NO LONGER CELEBRATING THE MAKAHIKI SEASON, THE HAWAIIANS WERE PERPLEXED BY THE RETURN OF THE MAN THEY ASSOCIATED WITH LONO, THE GOD OF THE MAKAHIKI. BECAUSE OF A DESIRE FOR IRON NAILS, SEVERAL NATIVES STOLE A CUTTER FROM ONE OF THE FOREIGNERS' SHIPS. COOK AND SEVERAL MARINES LANDED AND ATTEMPTED TO TAKE CHIEF KALANIOPU'U HOSTAGE IN EXCHANGE FOR THE RETURN OF THE BOAT. THEY HAD USED THIS STRATEGY SUCCESSFULLY IN TAHITI, BUT, AS THEY WERE ESCORTING KALANIOPU'U TO THE ROWBOAT, A SCUFFLE BROKE OUT. COOK SHOT AND KILLED A NATIVE, AND IN THE ENSUING FIGHT HE WAS KILLED. IT IS SAID THAT THE HAWAIIANS BURNED HIS BODY AND DIVIDED UP THE BONES. THIS MONUMENT WAS ERECTED IN 1874 BY THE BRITISH TO COMMEMORATE THE EVENT. THE EXACT SITE OF COOK'S DEATH IS NOW SUBMERGED.

THE PLACE OF REFUGE WAS A SANCTUARY FOR HAWAIIANS WHO HAD BROKEN *KAPU*. IF THEY COULD REACH THE SACRED GROUND, THEY WOULD ESCAPE PUNISHMENT FOR THIER CRIMES. THE ARTISTRY AND CRAFTSMANSHIP OF THE ANCIENT CULTURE ARE DISPLAYED IN THESE WOODEN *KI'I* OR GUARDIAN HAWAIIAN GODS THAT NOW PROTECT THE *HEIAU* AND THE ADJOINING STRUCTURES.

Adjoining the north end of the great wall is a reconstructed mausoleum *heiau*, Hale O Keawe. The chief's compound at Keoneʻele has a sandy cover that once was a canoe landing. Swimming and sunbathing are discouraged here.

Beyond the visitor center and parking lot, a short gravel road leads to the southern end of the *puʻuhonua* overlooking Alahaka Bay. This is an ideal place for snorkeling, picnicking, meditating, and taking a walk. The views through the coconut grove, with the great stony wall emanating some inarticulate *mana* (power), are sublime, especially at sunset or when illuminated by the moon.

Return to Mamalahoa Highway via Keokea and continue south to the Hoʻokena turnoff. A twisting two-mile road leads down to Hoʻokena Beach Park, where there is a gorgeous view of the sea cliffs of Kauhako Bay and the awesome (if featureless) slope of Mauna Loa as it dips to sea level. The beach is fine for swimming in normal weather. The near-shore snorkeling is excellent and easy to reach. The best spot is the rocky coast north of the old landing, formerly used to ship cattle from upland ranches. Hoʻokena port once boasted its own jail, courthouse, and school. Today, only a few families remain.

Hoʻokena ends the Kona tour. There are a few possible dinner spots on the drive back north in Captain Cook for family-style Japanese and American cuisine, and in Kainaliu, where fresh whole-grain fare is served in a cafe built in an old movie palace. Most local eating establishments close at 8 p.m.

✻ ✻ ✻ ✻

Magic Sands Beach on the Kona coast is one of the most stunning lava beaches on the Big Island.

THE VELVET GREENS OF THE MAUNA LANI RESORT'S 18-HOLE FRANCIS I'I BROWN CHAMPIONSHIP GOLF COURSE WEAVE THROUGH JAGGED 'A'A AND SMOOTH PAHOEHOE LAVA, CREATING A STUNNING CONTRAST OF COLORS AND TEXTURES.

KOHALA

THE MAIN HOTEL COMPLEX OF THE HILTON
WAIKOLOA VILLAGE ON THE KOHALA COAST IS SO
LARGE THAT THE QUICKEST WAY TO AND FROM YOUR
ROOM IS ABOARD THE BOATS IN THE LAGOON.

✳   ✳   ✳

THE DRIVE NORTH FROM Kailua-Kona along Queen Ka'ahumanu Highway into South Kohala is one of the island's most dazzling. North of the Keahole Airport, the air begins to clear of the Kona mist, and the huge, arid basin formed by the slopes of Hualālai, Mauna Loa, Mauna Kea, and Kohala takes shape across miles and miles of black lava. As it comes into focus, every element of the scruffy landscape gets bigger and bigger until it looks like Montana—except that one-half the view is of the infinite Pacific Ocean.

The road crests beyond Kuki'o on the flank of Hualālai. High above 'Alenuihaha Channel to the northwest, the lofty blue summit of Maui's Haleakalā shoulders above the clouds. Due north, the ragged shoreline stretches away for thirty miles to meet the sweep of Kohala as it enters the sea. The mottled slopes of Mauna Kea and Mauna Loa rise uninterrupted to glistening, frequently cloudless heights, two-and-a-half vertical miles above the shore.

Along the black coast there are occasional tufts of coconut and *kiawe* trees and a few small ponds barely visible behind the shore. The palm trees mark old settlements, fishponds, and beaches, some of which have been transformed into private home sites. Others are slated for resort development or public parks. At Ka'upulehu, thatched roofs amid the coconut trees mark the castaway-style of the Kona Village Resort. Down the road is the Four Seasons Resort at Hualalai, a hands-down favorties by honeymooners. Nearby, earth-moving equipment prepares the ground for more conventional resort hotels. Alongside the road, graffiti fashioned from bits of white coral enlivens the black-lava landscape.

The Kohala coast is the center of a resort boom that becomes increasingly apparent as the highway approaches the golf and beach havens at Waikoloa, Hapuna, Mauna Lani, and Mauna Kea—South Kohala's Gold Coast.

KAUNA'OA BEACH, ON THE GROUNDS OF MAUNA KEA BEACH HOTEL, IS ONE OF THE BIG ISLAND'S LOVELIEST SPOTS AND IS A FREQUENT NESTING PLACE FOR THE GREEN SEA TURTLE.

✻   ✻   ✻

All three "exclusive" resorts are open to casual visitors. Their wonderful beaches are, by law, public. The fishponds and petroglyph fields at 'Anaeho'omalu in Waikoloa and at Kalahuipua'a in the Mauna Lani Resort are significant and worthwhile historical sites. The glorious buffet at the Mauna Kea Beach Hotel is an institution and nearby is the beautiful Hapuna Beach Prince Hotel. The nightlife at the Outrigger Waikoloa Beach Resort is rowdy fun. The Hilton Waikoloa Village simply has to be seen to be believed.

As much as they are a trio, each resort is unique. At Waikoloa, the biggest and least exclusive of the three,

the sprawling estate is a living, breathing fantasy of extravagant excess: chances to swim with dolphins (by lottery and for a considerable fee) for 20 minutes; corridors choked with oversized art; seemingly endless pools with waterfalls and ersatz jungles; gondolas, monorails, fountains, more fountains. . . and a forlorn, artificial beach.

The more conventional Outrigger Waikoloa Beach Resort next door has wonderful 'Anaeho'omalu Beach at its front door, as well as some lovely historic fishponds.

A mile up the road, the luxurious, understated, elegant, and extremely expensive Mauna Lani Resort features bright-green golf courses, million-dollar condos, and two luxury hotels, the Mauna Lani Bay Hotel and Bungalows and the Orchid at Mauna Lani. The low-rise structures are spectacularly situated on rocky beaches close to Hawaiian fishponds. To reach the beach and fishponds, follow the resort's road signs to the "historical park," where there is free parking. A long, hot path across lava fields passes an ancient cave shelter. Archaeological remnants are marked and explained. The path eventually leads to the palm-shaded

ABOVE: PUʻUKOHOLA HEIAU, ABOVE KAWAIHAE BAY IN KOHALA, WAS BUILT IN 1791 BY KAMEHAMEHA IN HONOR OF HIS WAR GOD, KUKAʻILIMOKU.

LEFT: THE PARKER RANCH IN THE KOHALA DISTRICT OF THE BIG ISLAND IS A SERIES OF ROLLING GREEN PASTURES STRUNG TOGETHER WITH CLASSIC *PANIOLO* FENCES.

fishponds and rocky shorefront. The man-made hotel beach at Nanuku Inlet is to the right along the shore.

A few more miles up the road, the august and tasteful Mauna Kea Beach Hotel commands Kauna'oa Beach. A second hotel and golf course are planned. The Mauna Kea's fabulous beach is typical for this sunny stretch of coast. Others include the public beaches at Hapuna and Spencer Beach Park. On an island where beaches are rare, these three are deservedly popular.

UNLIKE THE OLDER ISLANDS OF MAUI, O'AHU, AND KAUA'I, THE BIG ISLAND, STILL IN ITS FORMATIVE PHASE, OFFERS FEW MATURE WHITE-SAND BEACHES. THE COVE AT HAPUNA BEACH PARK, ON THE KOHALA COAST, IS AN ARRESTING BREAK FROM THE SURROUNDING YOUNG, BLACK-LAVA LANDSCAPE.

✳   ✳   ✳

Pu'ukohola Heiau National Historical Site tops a prominent hill directly behind Spencer Beach Park. The impressive stone *heiau* was built in 1791 by Kamehameha to honor his war god, Kuka'ilimoku, and to ensure success in his campaign to subdue and unite the Hawaiian islands. Another, older *heiau*, Mailekini, lies adjacent to it. Park rangers at the National Parks Service Visitor Center have lots of stories about both sites.

The driest place in Hawai'i may be the port of Kawaihae, at the foot of the Kohala mountains. More utilitarian than attractive, its man-made beach built into the breakwater attracts windsurfers and families. The view back at Pu'ukohola from the *makai* (seaward) reaches of the breakwater is excellent.

P.S.: The waters south of the harbor, in front of Pu'ukohola, are famous as a shark-breeding area. The ruins of a third, submerged *heiau,* built by the Hawaiians to placate shark gods, are still out there.

The Kohala district really begins north of Kawaihae. It's a special corner of the island, the province of King Kamehameha, with some of Hawai'i's most sacred sites. At first glance the sites may look only like forlorn piles of rock; however, as your mind opens to their ancient significance, their power begins unmistakably to vibrate through the landscape.

Lapakahi State Historical Park, twelve miles north of Kawaihae on Route 270, is open daily (except Sunday) from 8 a.m. to 4 p.m. and offers a well-managed and evocative look at life in pre-contact Hawai'i. Here can be found the partially restored remnants of a 600-

SHAPED LIKE AN ARROW POINTING OUT TO SEA, THE MAUNA LANI BAY HOTEL AND BUNGALOWS IS LOCATED AMID 27 ACRES OF IMPORTANT HISTORIC SITES AND AT ONE OF THE KOHALA COAST'S MOST BEAUTIFUL BEACHES. THE HOTEL IS AN ACTIVE, FUNCTIONING EXAMPLE OF HAWAIIAN AQUACULTURE WITH ITS MAINTENANCE OF THE HOPEALA FISHPOND.

THE LAVA AND SAND SHORE OF THE KOHALA DISTRICT CAN BE VERY HARD ON THE FEET. WALK GINGERLY, WEAR SHOES, AND BE SURE TO STEP OVER THE LAVA.

year-old fishing village on the edge of the turquoise sea. A brochure guides you along the three-quarter-mile path through acres of archaeological remains and native flora. Low rock walls mark canoe sheds, communal house foundations, burial sites, and fishing shrines. The canoe landings at water's edge are bright, palm-shaded coves of white coral rubble. A few implements are scattered about, giving the appearance that the village's inhabitants had all gone fishing. The park's lively brochure encourages your imagination:

"What is the presence that is felt among these abandoned homes? Who is watching you pass between them? ... Find a shady rock and rest. Close your eyes and focus your mind on the shapes of stone. Surround yourself with the walls of Lapakahi as they are now—as they were centuries ago on the path ahead. You will feel the presence—you will look for things which are but cannot be seen."

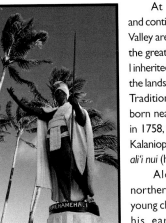

In the late 1870's, when the Hawaiian Kingdom commissioned an Italian artist to complete a statue of Kamehameha the Great, the people of Kohala requested that it be placed near his birthplace in the district of Kohala on the island of Hawai'i. The ship carrying the statue from Italy to Hawai'i sank off the Falkland Islands. A second statue was sent in its place and was dedicated in Honolulu at the time of King Kalaukaua's coronation in 1882. A few years later, the original statue was salvaged and sold to the Hawaiian government. Today it stands in Kohala near Kamehameha's first home.

*   *   *

Just north of Lapakahi is picturesque Mahukona landing, a great spot for a dip in the sea (there are showers).

At 'Upolu Point and continuing to Pololu Valley are the lands that the great Kamehameha I inherited, in contrast to the lands he conquered. Tradition says he was born near 'Upolu Point in 1758, the nephew of Kalaniopu'u, the island's *ali'i nui* (highest chief).

Along Kohala's northern reaches, the young chief performed his early feats. He carved a rock path down a vertical lava sea cliff to haul up his canoe from the small bay at Kapanaia for safe keeping. Unlike most other chiefs, he irrigated and cultivated his own fields. He is said to have carried, just for sport, a trunk-size boulder miles up a valley from the beach. "Kamehameha's Rock" lies at the edge of Highway 270 on a hairpin turn east of Kapa'au. William Ellis, an early English missionary, reporting on his tour of the island in 1823, commented that "great undertakings appear to have been [Kamehameha's]

Near Waikoloa, the Puako Petroglyphs (one of the largest petroglyph fields on the island) are carved on *pahoehoe* lava. Considered some of the earliest human artifacts, these Hawaiian petroglyphs were chiseled into smooth lava shelves along the ancient trail. This particular picture is of a man carrying a staff, spear, or banner.

Above: Kamuela Museum, an independent memorial to the Parker Ranch lifestyle of the early 1900s, is an eclectic collection of ancient Hawaiian tools and antique American and Chinese furniture. This sitting room, decorated in turn-of-the-century Hawaiian-style opulence, is filled with *koa* and wicker furniture, a crystal chandelier, an open-beamed ceiling, and a fireplace to ward off the damp chill of the upland evenings.

Left: Tradition says that the Mo'okini Heiau was constructed around A.D. 480 by the legendary *kahuna* Pa'ao. In a single night, thousands of basalt stones were moved hand to hand by a human chain from Pololu Valley, 12 miles north, to the temple site.

delight, and achievements deemed by others impracticable were those which he regarded as most suitable exercises of his prowess." (*The Journal of William Ellis* by William Ellis).

Turn *makai* (seaward) off the highway at the signs for 'Upolu Airport for a short drive to 'Upolu Point and the Mo'okini Heiau at the island's northernmost reach. At the end of the dirt road beyond the *heiau* is where Kamehameha is said to have been born. The group of smooth rocks—traditional birthstones rising out of the red earth—is enclosed in a low rock wall. A few hundred yards to the east is Mo'okini Heiau, believed to have been built in the fifth century and rebuilt in the fifteenth century by Pa'ao, a legendary white *kahuna* (priest).

Mo'okini is one of Hawai'i's great *heiau* and certainly one of its most primal, sacred spots. The wind-swept meadow at the edge of sea cliffs is backed by the Kohala Mountains and oriented northward across the blustery 'Alenuihaha Channel to the dark shores of Kaupo and Hana on Maui. The thickset rectangular *luakini* (human

THE GREEN HILLS AND FERTILE PASTURES OF THE KAMUELA AREA ARE HOME TO MANY OF THE BIG ISLAND'S CATTLE AND HORSE RANCHES. *PANIOLO*, OR HAWAIIAN COWBOYS, HERD THEIR LIVESTOCK THROUGH GREEN UPLAND MEADOWS INTO CORRALS FOR BRANDING, MUCH LIKE THEY HAVE DONE FOR WELL OVER A CENTURY. THE BIG ISLAND RANCHES PARTICIPATE IN THE HAWAI'I RODEO CIRCUIT, HOLDING ANNUAL ROUNDUPS AND COMPETITIONS TO TEST AND HONE THE SKILLS OF THESE HARDWORKING *PANIOLO*.

*　　　*　　　*

sacrifice) *heiau* was dedicated to the war god Ku, to whom human sacrifices were made. The *heiau's* location is fitting, considering the enmity between the chiefs of Hawai'i and Maui, and the endless war canoes launched across these treacherous waters.

Kohala, Hawi, and Kapa'au are old plantation settlements full of local charm and picturesque gardens. At Kapa'au, a stately Victorian-era statue of King Kamehameha gestures to passing cars. The highway ends at the Pololu Overlook, which has a splendid view down to the gray Pololu beach and the inaccessible cliffs and valleys of windward Kohala. A mildly strenuous hike leads down to Pololu Valley's beach and brings you back again in about ninety minutes. The trailhead is at the far end of the parking area. Don't plan to swim. The surf is normally treacherous.

The twenty-five-mile "High Road" southward from Hawi climbs the rolling crest of the Kohala ridge, then descends into the ranch town of Kamuela. It's another of the Big Island's spectacular drives, particularly at sunset or under a full moon. It crosses some incredibly green grasslands with views of the

MALE AND FEMALE *PA'U* RIDERS ADD ELEGANCE AND GRACE TO THE FESTIVITIES AND SPECTACLE OF THE KAMEHAMEHA DAY PARADE.

A SOFT WASH OF YELLOW MORNING LIGHT BRIGHTENS THE PROTESTANT CHURCH IN WAIMEA. BETWEEN THE YEARS OF 1838 AND 1840, DURING THE ISLAND-WIDE "GREAT REVIVAL," MORE THAN 20,000 NATIVE CONVERTS WERE TAKEN INTO THE FOLD, LARGELY DUE TO THE EFFORTS OF BROTHER LORENZO LYONS, THE MINISTER OF THIS LITTLE CONGREGATION.

biggest landscape on earth. Don't, under any circumstances, miss this drive. (The Kohala Mountain Road is also known as Highway 250.)

Kamuela, or Waimea, is an upscale ranch and farming center, home of the *paniolo* (Hawaiian cowboy) and headquarters for the 225,000-acre Parker Ranch and a few other large cattle spreads. Waimea, meaning "red water," is the ancient Hawaiian name for the area. Kamuela is a Hawaiianization of Samuel, a name given to the town in the nineteenth century in honor of Samuel Parker, patriarch of the prominent ranching family.

This cool, green town, perched 2,600 feet above the Kohala desert at the leeward edge of the perpetual Waipi'o rain clouds, is becoming a haven for the affluent. Fine restaurants are tucked into old houses, and shopping arcades serve a clientele from the nearby South Kohala resorts. Art galleries occupy old stables. Ranch owners sell chunks of their choicest lands for million-dollar vacation homes with billion-dollar views. Polo is a popular spectator sport.

Kamuela is also home to two of the state's most eccentric museums. The Kamuela Museum, at the intersection of Highways 250 and 19, is owned by Albert and Harriet Solomon, old-timers who have collected a dizzying assortment of Hawaiian artifacts, as well as an incredible hodge-podge of historical memorabilia and kitsch from all over the world. All of it is carefully pre-sented and ex-plained on type-written labels. Harriet Solomon is a member of the Parker ranching family; Portuguese-Hawaiian Albert's grandmother, a member of the *kahuna* class, predicted that he would one day have a place where the whole world would visit. The Solomons charge a small admission fee to peruse their life's work.

Harriet Solomon's cousin, Richard Smart, inherited the 225,000-acre Parker Ranch. Actually, he inherited more land than that but sold off several large tracts, including the 31,000 acres of today's Waikoloa Resort. As a young man, Smart had a career on Broadway. His suave voice on thirty-year-old recordings can be heard during a tour of his 100-year-old ranch house/museum/home at Pu'uopelu. Outside, the home is simple; inside it's "American in Paris," circa 1955. French paintings, including canvasses by Boudin, Degas, and Corot, line the pale

AT SUNSET, ANAEHO'OMALU BAY IS DISTINGUISHED BY THE EXTENSIVE COCONUT GROVE THAT FRINGES TWO FISHPONDS AND A LONG, CURVING WHITE-SAND BEACH. ANAEHO'OMALU IS ONE OF THE MOST EXQUISITE BEACHES ON THE KOHALA COAST AND IS PART OF THE OUTRIGGER WAIKOLOA BEACH HOTEL COMPLEX.

✷   ✷   ✷

THE PARKER RANCH HOUSE, THE PRIVATE RESIDENCE OF THE LAST DESCENDANT OF SAMUEL PARKER, WAS RECENTLY OPENED TO THE PUBLIC AS A HISTORIC MUSEUM. AS PART OF THE RANCH COMPLEX, THIS MODEST STRUCTURE OFFERS AN EXCELLENT COLLECTION OF PRIVATELY-OWNED ART TREASURES AND THE MEMENTOS OF ONE OF THE OLDEST AND MOST AFFLUENT NON-HAWAIIAN FAMILIES IN THIS ISLAND'S HISTORY.

walls. Chintz and brocade-upholstered furniture, Ming vases, and thick carpets give a continental hush to the big, skylit rooms. French doors lead to a formal French garden. Personal effects (note pads, personal portraits, magazines, and his TV remote control) reveal that Smart actually lived in the house, which is open to the public Tuesday through Saturday from 11 a.m. to 4:15 p.m. for a small admission fee. Also open for viewing is the reconstructed house of John Parker, the ranch's founder and Smart's great-great-grandfather. Originally built in 1840, the home features an interior of solid *koa* wood.

Parker Ranch offers extended van tours of the entire ranch. Starting at the Visitor Center in the Parker Ranch Shopping Center, they include trips to the house at Puʻuopelu, the historic mountainside homestead at Mana, the Parker family cemetery, and various working areas of the ranch, including the Puʻukalani stable, where you can meet some real *paniolo* (cowboys). The story of the Parker family dynasty and how its vast landholdings were consolidated is fascinating.

Among Kamuela's notable restaurants are Edelweiss, a small Swiss inn with a meaty menu; Merriman's, where fresh local produce gets the nouvelle cuisine touch from an ambitious young chef; Hartwell's, for hearty meat and game dishes served in the cozy rooms of a former ranch manager's house; and the Paniolo Country Inn, a family restaurant for barbecue, pizza, and burgers.

Two small hotels in Kamuela offer a cool night's sleep. They are the renovated Kamuela Inn, now a charming spot with free continental breakfast; and the recently redecorated motel-style Parker Ranch Lodge, at the center of town. Both are very busy places on weekends.

THE MASSIVE, SNOW-CAPPED VISTA OF MAUNA KEA, THE "WHITE MOUNTAIN," LOOMS ABOVE THE SMALL COMMUNITY OF WAIMEA, THE HEART OF *PANIOLO* COUNTRY.

THE PLACID DEEP BLUE WATER OF REED'S BAY IN HILO
HAS BECOME A POPULAR BOATING HARBOR. YACHTS
ANCHOR NEAR THE FAMOUS BANYAN DRIVE, A
SEMICIRCULAR ROAD SHADED BY MASSIVE INDIAN
BANYANS. ON THE NORTH POINT OF THE WAIKEA
PENINSULA STANDS THE IMPOSING NANILOA HOTEL, AND
TUCKED INTO THE SHORELINE IS WAILOA STATE PARK
WITH THE BEAUTIFULLY LANDSCAPED JAPANESE-STYLE
LILI'UOKALANI GARDEN.

HAMAKUA AND HILO

THE DRIVE FROM KOHALA to Hilo passes along the Big Island's windward Hamakua coast, with its sea cliffs, broad fields of sugar cane, and ravines that drain off the incessant rains that fall on Mauna Kea's windward highlands. Hamakua's northeastern end—where the deep valleys of Waipi'o, Waimanu, Honopue, Honoke'a, Honokane Iki, Honokane, and Pololu create a spectacular and mostly inaccessible landscape—is the most heavily-eroded portion of the geologically young Big Island.

Start the tour at Waipi'o Valley, reachable by car from Kona and Kohala via Highway 19 through Kamuela to Honoka'a, and west on Highway 240 to the Waipi'o Valley overlook. Spend a few minutes gazing at the valley.

Early in the nineteenth century, when the valley was a thriving center of Hawaiian civilization, an English visitor, standing where you are now, wrote these observations:

"Viewed from the great elevation at which we stood, the charming valley, spread out beneath us like a map, with its numerous inhabitants, cottages, plantations, fishponds, and meandering streams, (on the surface of which the light canoe was moving to and fro), appeared in beautiful miniature.

"…The next morning unveiled to view the extent and beauty of the romantic valley …The bottom of the valley was one continuous garden, cultivated with taro, bananas, sugar-cane, and other productions of the islands, all growing luxuriantly. Several large ponds were also seen in different directions, well stocked with excellent fish. A number of small villages, containing from twenty to fifty houses each, stood along the foot of the mountains, at unequal distances on each side, and extended up the valley till projecting cliffs obstructed the view."

from *The Journal of William Ellis*

Today, population and cultivation are drastically reduced at Waipiʻo, but its beauty and romance endure. The road to the valley floor is open only to hikers and four-wheel-drive vehicles. Ninety-minute shuttle bus tours are available

TAHITIAN LIMES DECORATED FOR IMMEDIATE SALE, ALONGSIDE AVOCADO, KONA ORANGES, AND PERSIMMONS, ARE A PART OF THE DAILY DISPLAY OF LOCAL GROWN FRUITS AND VEGETABLES AT THE HILO OPEN MARKET.

✳   ✳   ✳

that leave from the lookout area. Direct-line phones at the lookout allow you to reserve seats on the next shuttle. The walk down is easy, but it's a strenuous climb back up.

Honokaʻa is headquarters for the recently defunct Hamakua Sugar Company, the last of the big plantations in Hamakua to hold out against low sugar prices, high labor costs, the threat of an end to U.S. sugar subsidies, and difficult growing conditions among the deeply-cut ravines of the Hamakua coast.

Macadamia orchards have replaced some of the sugar cane; the Hawaiian Holiday Macadamia Nut Company runs tours of a macadamia nut factory in town. Honokaʻa Town is western/plantation architecture, perilously perched above the

Pacific. A side road leads down the hill to Haina sugar mill, where cane was squeezed and boiled into molasses or raw sugar. Just beyond the mill is the landing where, in the old days, the mo-lasses was delivered to ships through a hose.

East of Honokaʻa, Highway 19 follows the old, miraculously engineered railroad line with hundreds of bridges, which carried both sugar and passengers across countless streams and gorges between Honokaʻa and Hilo. Plantation towns dot the landscape: Laupahoehoe, Papaʻaloa, Honomu, Pepeʻekeo, Papaʻikou ....Today the towns are just shadows of their glory days, when sugar was king and thousands of workers from China, Japan, Portugal, and the Philippines turned quiet native villages into cosmopolitan festivals of Buddhist observance, Portuguese music, Hawaiian ghost stories, and Chinese food. Mechanization and shrinking sugar acreage sent many younger residents off to Hilo, Honolulu, and even to the U.S. mainland for better wages and opportunities.

The chief attractions along this scenic coast, besides the colorful

THE BIG ISLAND BLOOMS
AS THE CAPITAL OF THE
HAWAIIAN FLOWER
INDUSTRY. VENDORS
PEDDLE THEIR WHITE, PINK,
CORAL, AND DRAMATIC
RED ANTHURIUMS.

ISOLATED BY SHEER CLIFFS AND A CHURNING BAY OF TWISTING CURRENTS, WAIPI'O VALLEY HAS BEEN ABLE TO REMAIN
ONE OF THE LAST VESTIGES OF A HAWAI'I TIED TO THE *'AINA*, THE LAND.

plantation towns, are the rugged beauty of Laupahoehoe Point, picture-postcard 'Akaka Falls, intimate Kolekole Beach Park, and the cultivated splendor of Hawai'i Tropical Botanical Garden at Onomea Bay.

From Wai-pi'o to Hilo, the Hamakua sea cliffs are un-interrupted, except at Laupa-hoehoe Point, where a wide, flat tongue of lava juts into the turbulent sea. In the old days, Laupahoehoe's canoe landing made it a popular stop for seafarers journeying by canoe or steamship between Hilo and Kohala.

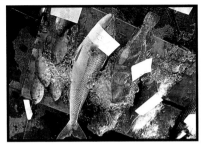
COMMERCIAL FISHERMEN SUPPLY THE LOCAL RESTAURANTS WITH DAILY SUPPLIES OF FRESH-CATCH DELICACIES.
✻   ✻   ✻

But Laupahoehoe is best known for a tragedy. On April 1, 1946, thirty-two persons, many of them pupils in a school on the point, perished during a catastrophic *tsunami*, or tidal wave. Successive waves reaching heights of thirty feet destroyed the school as they scoured the low-lying point. A memorial stone marks the school site, now a scenic, but melancholy, beach park.

The surf crashing on the rocks is gorgeous to watch, but swimming anywhere on the point is not recommended. The road to Laupahoehoe, about midway between Honoka'a and Hilo, is clearly marked on the road to 'Akaka Falls State Park. The falls are celebrated in songs and legends and, like the Grand Canyon, simply have to be seen. The area surrounding the 442-foot plunge of Kolekole Stream resembles a rain forest in Eden, but it is, in fact, one of Hawai'i's most mature and skillfully designed public gardens, created in the 1920s by Bill Bryan, an obscure district forester.

Kolekole Stream enters the ocean a few miles downstream from 'Akaka Falls, at Kolekole Beach Park, the prettiest—and safest—place for a swim between Kawaihae and Hilo (see Beaches).

At Pepe'ekeo, turn *makai*, (seaward), off the highway to Pepe'ekeo Point for a great view and a look at the local sugar mill. Then, rather than return to the highway, head toward Hilo on what is called the Pepe'ekeo Scenic Drive, a winding, four-mile road through old-time Hamakua. Hilo Bay and the long, sloping ridge of the Kīlauea east rift zone are clearly visible twenty miles to the south. If the volcano is erupting and the weather is right, you should be able to see volcanic smoke above the active vents on the distant ridge line.

At Onomea Bay, the Hawai'i Tropical Botanical Garden, self-billed as "the most beautiful area in Hawai'i," is a private, nonprofit, twenty-acre garden

NAMED AFTER HAWAI'I'S ONLY FEMALE MONARCH, QUEEN LILI'UOKALANI, THIS 30-ACRE PARK IN HILO WITH ITS RED JAPANESE BRIDGE, STONE SCULPTURES, TEA CEREMONY PAGODA, AND TRANQUIL FOOTPATHS, REFLECTS THE HERITAGE BROUGHT TO THIS AREA BY JAPANESE IMMIGRANTS.

THE BREATHTAKING VISTAS AND PLUMMETING WATERFALLS OF THE HAMAKUA COAST HAVE GIVEN RISE TO MANY MYTHS, CHANTS, AND *HULAS*. THE HAWAIIAN PROVERB PRAISING THE VALLEYS AND CLIFFS OF THIS MAJESTIC LAND IS "HAMAKUA I KA WAKAWAKA," ("IRREGULAR AND ROUGH HAMAKUA").

where, for a fee, you are bused from the visitor center to the gardens and given a map. Once inside, you can stroll at your own pace through a palm forest hosting a thousand tropical plant species from around the world. The garden is never crowded; visitors are limited to about 150 a day.

The last stop on this tour is Hilo, a dowdy, old-fashioned place, set in a perpetual garden. More than any other place in Hawai'i, Hilo has the lingering romantic feel of a South Pacific town, with simple architecture, a humid, slow-paced attitude, and lots of greenery.

THE BRIGHT COLORS OF A RAINBOW HOVER IN THE MISTS NEAR THE BASE OF 'AKAKA FALLS. PROTECTED AND CARED FOR BY THE STATE PARKS SYSTEM, WATER FROM THE UPLANDS SPLASHES 442 FEET INTO A TROPICAL RAIN FOREST OF GIANT GINGER, HELICONIA, FERNS, ORCHIDS, AND BAMBOO. WHEN A NEARBY STONE CALLED POHAKU O PELE (STONE OF PELE) IS STRUCK BY A LEHUA 'APANE BRANCH, THE SKY DARKENS AND RAIN FALLS.

It's a sober, real town, blessedly free of both pseudo-sophistication and self-conscious quaintness.

Hilo is a collection of neighborhoods. The amazingly intact, vintage downtown is worth a stroll. Some of Hilo's best restaurants, bars, and shops are tucked behind the area's painted wood-and-stucco facades. Park along the waterfront on Kamehameha Avenue close to Waianuenue Avenue and have a drink or a meal, or walk a block to Keawe Street, where a number of trendy spots have put the "oh!" back in Hilo A short drive four blocks up Waianuenue Avenue and then down Haili Street passes several of Hilo's impressive pre-World War II buildings, including the public library with two historic stones, the lovely grounds of Hilo High School and the Federal Building, the old police station, and Hawaiian Telephone Building, all facing Kalakaua Park. On Haili Street, the Lyman House Museum and Haili Church (1824) bring Hilo's missionary past into sharp focus.

Despite several devastating tsunamis (the worst were in 1946 and 1960), Hilo manages to survive and prosper without too many tourists or too many hotels. It is the flower-growing and agricultural capital of the state and still the commercial and political headquarters for the Big Island, despite the challenge from booming Kona.

After decades of furious growth elsewhere, the rest of Hawai'i is beginning to take rainy Hilo seriously.

LAUPAHOEHOE OR "LEAF OF SMOOTH LAVA" IS A PENINSULA ON THE HAMAKUA COAST. IN LEGEND, THIS FLAT SPIT OF LAND WAS THE RESULT OF A *HOLUA* (DRY-LAND SLEDDING) CONTEST THAT TURNED INTO A VIOLENT BATTLE BETWEEN THE SNOW GODDESS POLI'AHU AND THE VOLCANO GODDESS PELE. THE FIERCELY JEALOUS PELE RAGED OVER POLI'AHU'S ATHLETIC SKILL IN THE SPORT OF SLEDDING AND THE ATTENTION GIVEN TO HER BY THE SPECTATORS. PELE SENT A LAVA FLOW TO DESTROY POLI'AHU'S HOME ON MAUNA KEA. POLI'AHU DIVERTED THE ERUPTION BY SENDING SNOW AND COLD WINDS TO REROUTE THE MOLTEN RIVER THROUGH LAUPAHOEHOE GULCH AND INTO THE SEA.

FEW PEOPLE JOURNEY TO THE HEADWATERS OF THE RIVERS THAT ERODE RAVINES AND VALLEYS ON THEIR WAY TO THE SEA. WITH PERMISSION FROM NEIGHBORING RANCHERS TO UNLOCK THEIR GATES, OCCASIONAL HUNTERS AND FORESTERS RIDE THEIR JEEPS AND HORSES UP INTO THE BACK COUNTRY OF THE LAUPAHOEHOE FOREST RESERVE. HERE THE TALL *KOA* AND *'OHI'A* TREES STAND ALONGSIDE FERNS AND DWARF PALMS IN THE RAIN FOREST MIST OF SUMMER.

The watery Waiakea district, site of Hilo's original Hawaiian settlement, includes hotel row along Banyan Drive (shaded by a row of banyans planted by famous visitors), Bayfront Park, and the Wailoa River State Recreation Area. The two parks, established on lands previously devastated by *tsunamis*, also serve as buffers against future seismic surf.

This entire area is worth a good, long walk. Of special note are the Japanese gardens in Lili'uokalani Park and picturesque Coconut Island, reachable by a foot bridge from the seaward end of Waiakea peninsula. These are among Hilo's most photographed and idyllic spots. The thirty serene acres at Lili'uokalani Gardens pay tribute to Hilo's important Japanese-American community. It is the largest Japanese garden of its type outside Japan. In former times Coconut Island was an important *pu'uhonua* (site of healing and refuge) called Mokuola, "island of life."

RAINBOW FALLS (OR WAIANUINUI) IN THE WAILUKU RIVER SHIMMERS IN PRISMATIC WONDER WHEN BLESSED BY THE SUN IN THE EARLY MORNING AND LATE AFTERNOON HOURS. A CAVE BEHIND THE CASCADING WATER IS SAID TO HAVE BEEN THE HOME OF HINA, MOTHER OF MĀUI THE DEMIGOD. THE HILO AREA IS KNOWN FOR ITS FREQUENT RAINFALL, AVERAGING 133 INCHES A YEAR. WATER WAS SO ESSENTIAL TO THE WELL-BEING OF A VILLAGE THAT THE HAWAIIAN WORD FOR WEALTH IS *WAIWAI*, ABUNDANT WATER.

✻   ✻   ✻

Recommended driving tours of Hilo include a trip along Kalaniana'ole Avenue to the string of beach parks lining the easternmost reaches of Hilo Bay. The views are great, and these rocky shorefronts feel like places where the unique Polynesian relationship between man and ocean has never been interrupted. The beach parks include Onekahakaha Beach Park, James Kealoha Beach Park, Leleiwi Beach Park, and, at the end of the road, Lehia Beach Park.

A quick tour of Hilo's neighborhoods unveils marvelous little gardens and neat, tin-roofed houses that are domestic Hilo's pride and joy. Take Waianuenue Avenue up to the Kaumana Drive turn-off and just drive around, oohing and aahing until you get lost.

MAUNA KEA, CLASSIFIED AS DORMANT, RISES TO 13,796 FEET ABOVE SEA LEVEL AND IS THE WORLD'S LARGEST MOUNTAIN, IF YOU CAN COUNT THE THOUSANDS OF FEET IT DESCENDS TO THE OCEAN FLOOR. GEOLOGISTS THEORIZE THAT IN THE LAST ICE AGE GLACIERS SLITHERED DOWN THE SLOPES. GLACIAL MORAINES AND PERMAFROST BENEATH THE ROCKY CRUST REMAIN TODAY. THE VIEW OF A SNOW-CAPPED MOUNTAIN THROUGH WAVING PALM FRONDS SEEMS AN INCONGRUOUS IMAGE, ESPECIALLY TO FIRST-TIME VISITORS WHOSE PRECONCEPTIONS OF HAWAI'I DON'T INCLUDE THIS VISION OF PARADISE.

FIERY STREAMS OF RED-ORANGE LAVA SPILL
INTO THE OCEAN AND GENERATE PLUMING
CLOUDS OF WHITE HISSING STEAM. THE
MEETING OF SEA AND FIRE HURLS SMALL DROPS
OF STILL-MOLTEN LAVA HIGH INTO THE AIR. THE
VOLCANIC GLASS INSTANTLY COOLS AS TINY
GRAINS, WHICH ACCUMULATE TO FORM
HAWAI'I'S FAMED BLACK-SAND BEACHES.

THE VOLCANO & PUNA

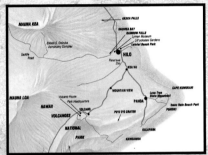

On January 3, 1983, the southeastern flank of Kīlauea Volcano erupted. It spewed out nearly 650,000 cubic yards of lava every 24 hours.

❈   ❈   ❈

If you are coming from the distant Kona and Kohala resort areas, there are two approaches to Hawai'i Volcanoes National Park. Via Hamakua and Hilo, the drive is 115 miles—a little over two hours; going around South Point it's 125 miles and takes about two-and-a-half hours. Choosing your route depends on what you have already seen of the island. The Hamakua-Hilo route has a better road surface.

Hawai'i Volcanoes National Park

After Honolulu's U.S. National Memorial Cemetery of the Pacific (Punchbowl), Hawai'i Volcanoes National Park is the busiest visitor destination in the State. In 1998, well more than two million came to peer into the guts of creation.

The National Park entrance is within a mile of the summit of Kīlauea, the world's most accessible active volcano, a broad 4,000-foot shoulder on Mauna Loa's eastern slope. The Visitor Center is your essential first stop. Pamphlets and maps will get you oriented. Helpful rangers will give you the latest news on volcanic activity. Please have patience if they tell you there's no way to see current lava flows except by helicopter. You are probably the thousandth person they've had to disappoint that day.

Within a few miles of the Visitor Center are the Park's most popular attractions, including the Volcano Art Center, lookout points with informative signs, the Thurston Lava Tube, Devastation Trail, Halema'uma'u Crater, and Jaggar Museum at the Volcano Observatory. Each is strongly recommended for a visit.

With a certain amount of vigor, these can be covered in about three hours. They're all on Crater Rim Drive, which circles Kīlauea Caldera, the summit's single most impressive feature. Within the "drive-in caldera" are a patchwork of recent lava flows and rift zones in various shades of black and gray, steaming sulfur fissures, and the famous Halema'uma'u firepit, a deep, circular crater that occasionally contains a fountaining pool of lava. As Mark Twain observed during his visit to Kīlauea, "The smell of sulfur is strong, but not unpleasant to a sinner."

Halema'uma'u is also the home of Pele, the fire goddess. Offerings of flowers, ti leaves, and bottles of gin are often left at the edge of the firepit by her followers.

The Jaggar Museum at the Volcano Observatory should not be missed. It's a new and delightful presentation of everything you ever thought you'd want to know about geology and volcanology. The expansive views from the terrace outside the museum are the best in the park.

Hawai'i Volcanoes National Park covers 200,000 acres on Kīlauea and Mauna Loa, stretching down to the shore to include thirty miles of coastline. After the Kīlauea summit itself, the park's most spectacular area is Kīlauea's eastward slope, a 4,000-foot descent to the sea over the Chain of Craters Road, another of the Big Island's awesome scenic drives. A seaward section of the road was cut by lava flows in the late 1980s, so you will have to turn around when you reach it. The round-trip drive takes about two hours, including brief stops for picture-taking.

The excellent twenty-four-mile road passes several pit craters (thus its name), then emerges from the 'ohi'a forest onto the vast black fields of twenty-year-old lava that flowed from scenic Mauna Ulu, a mini-mountain on Kīlauea's pockmarked East Rift. Suddenly, the terrain steepens dramatically and the road looks like it's going to dive right off the Holei pali (cliff) into the blue sea below. At the bottom of the precipice,

DEVASTATION TRAIL, IS NOW A PAVED PATH THROUGH VOLCANOES NATIONAL PARK.

❈   ❈   ❈

THE THURSTON LAVA TUBE, NAMED FOR THE MISSIONARY THURSTON FAMILY, IS A COOL SUBTERRANEAN TUNNEL IN THE MIDST OF JUNGLE FERNS. THE OLD NAME, NAHAKU, MEANS "THE PROTURBERANCES."

LAVA TREE STATE PARK IN PAHOA WAS FORMED BY AN ADVANCING *PAHOEHOE* LAVA FLOW. STILL LIQUID, THE LAVA WRAPPED AND COVERED THE TREES AND FERNS OF THE UPLAND RAIN FOREST, MOLDING WEIRD SHAPES AROUND THE CHARRED TRUNKS.

COCONUT TREES LINE A COUNTRY ROAD ALONG THE JAGGED PUNA COASTLINE. THE ʻAʻA LAVA THAT FORMED THIS DRAMATIC LANDSCAPE IS THE HEAD OF AN ANCIENT FLOW THAT COOLED WHEN IT HIT THE SEA.

safely negotiated via one long switchback, the view back at the *pali* reveals the innumerable layers of lava that have poured down its face. It's one of Hawai'i's most arresting and impressive geological sights.

Eventually the road reaches the shore and heads east to Waha'ula, where in 1989 the road, the Park Visitor Center, and a nearby *heiau* were covered by lava. Along the way back, there are several

ALTHOUGH *TI* LEAVES, FLOWERS, AND GILBEY'S GIN LEFT ON THE LAVA ROCKS AT HAWAI'I VOLCANOES NATIONAL PARK ARE ACCEPTABLE OFFERINGS TO PELE, THE PARK DOES PREFER THAT VISITORS TREAT THE AREAS WITH THE GREATEST RESPECT BY NOT LEAVING ANYTHING BEHIND.

✻   ✻   ✻

options for short hiking trips and scenic sites. A rather large, palm-fringed, gray-sand beach near the end of the road at Kamoamoa has some marked archaeological sites, including a canoe house. There are restrooms, camp-grounds, and the services of a park ranger. On the shore, the sea has carved two sea arches into the low lava cliffs at Holei and Nāulu.

The petroglyph field at Pu'u Loa is one of Hawai'i's most extensive. The one-mile trail to the petroglyphs is marked on the road near the base of the Holei *pali*. Be sure you have water; the walk is easy, but it can get very hot.

If you have more time, there's an extensive network of hiking trails in the summit area and along the coast. Check at the Visitor Center for details.

Overnight campers must register at the Park Service Headquarters.

Lunch and dinner options in and around the park include the historic Volcano House over-looking Kīlauea Caldera (at lunch this place is packed with bus tours); the Volcano Golf and Country Club Rest-aurant; and Kīlauea Lodge for fine dinners in the neighboring town of Volcano.

The District of Puna

Lohi'au Puna i ke akua wahine.
Weliweli 'ino Puna i ke akua wahine.
Ke lauahi maila o Pele ia Puna.
Puna is set back because of the goddess.
Puna is terrified of the goddess.
Pele is pouring lava out on Puna.
        —*a Puna district folk saying*

Puna long has borne the brunt of Pele's fury. Lava flows originating on Kīlauea's East Rift have been wiping out villages and creating new black-sand beaches with a regularity that should discourage habitation. Yet people continue to set up homes between the flows and hope that they will be spared.

Pele's most recent victims have been the much photographed black-sand beaches at Kalapana and Kaimu.

PAHOEHOE LAVA CREEPS ACROSS A PUNA HIGHWAY IN THE ROYAL GARDENS SUBDIVISION NEAR KALAPANA DURING THE 1992 KĪLAUEA VOLCANIC ERUPTION. WHEN LAVA CROSSES A ROAD, THE ASPHALT CATCHES FIRE, RELEASING OILY BLACK SMOKE CLOUDS. HEAT WAVES WARP AND TWIST LINES OF SIGHT ALONG ITS RIPPLING HOT SURFACE.

'OHI'A AND FERN FORESTS COVER THE SLOPES OF MAUNA LOA AND SEEM TO TEMPT PELE'S WRATH WITH THEIR VIBRANT RESILIENCE AND PERSISTENCE. WITH EACH ERUPTION, PORTIONS OF THE FORESTS ARE BURNED AND BURIED UNDER THE HEAT AND WEIGHT OF PELE'S LAVA.

Gone, too, is the fondly remembered village of Kalapana, its 200 homes, a beach park, surf sites, a store, and two churches.

In contrast to Puna's barren lava fields are nearby areas where papaya, macadamia nuts, orchids, oranges, and anthuriums thrive in mineral-rich earth that has avoided volcanic inundation over hundreds of years.

To reach Puna, follow Highway 11 out of Hilo and turn left at Kea'au. Highway 130 leads into Pahoa, an old hippie town and "capital" of Puna, almost a separate kingdom. A strong countercultural current pervades the rural community where marijuana cultivation has been a lucrative activity, despite official efforts to stamp it out. Puna is also where a business-government consortium has tapped volcanic heat to produce geothermal energy. Some Hawaiian-rights activists and environmentalists oppose the project and large-scale demonstrations have occurred.

To complicate matters, those who recognize the ancient Hawaiian belief system say that Pele, the goddess of fire inhabiting the volcano, will be physically assaulted by geothermal drilling, tapping, and injecting, and that ultimately geothermal energy production will pollute the volcano, sap its strength, and force Pele to leave Kīlauea.

A KAHILI GINGER RISES WITH TALISMANIC MAJESTY IN THE DEPTHS OF THE RAIN FOREST.

✳   ✳   ✳

To view the recent lava flows at Kaimu and Kalapana, continue south from Pahoa on Highway 130 to where the lava flows prevent further travel. From an elevated vantage point, the newest flows to the sea are clearly visible. Closer viewing is sometimes possible.

A drive back along the Puna coast on Highway 137 all the way to Cape Kumukahi—if lava flows permit—completes the Puna tour. MacKenzie State Recreation Area, Isaac Hale Beach Park (with naturally heated freshwater pools) at Pohoiki Bay, and scenic Kehena Beach (see Beaches) are popular stops.

Highways 137 and 132 intersect near Cape Kumukahi. The road to the cape is a desolate drive to an abandoned lighthouse at the easternmost point in the Hawaiian islands. The nearby village of Kapoho was covered by black lava in 1960 after a vent opened less than a half mile above the town. By the time the devastating, month-long eruption was over, it had built the 450-foot Kapoho cinder cone, which now dominates the area. Toxic fumes from the eruption veiled the sun throughout the Hawaiian chain and killed plants as far away as O'ahu.

HAPU'U FERNS AND *'OHI'A* BUSHES BRAVELY GROW ON THE RIMS OF CRATERS IN HAWAI'I VOLCANOES NATIONAL PARK. HALEMA'UMA'U (THE HOUSE OF FERNS) CRATER IS NAMED AFTER THESE *'AMA'U* FERNS THAT THRIVE IN THE SULFUR-RICH AIR AND CLING TO THE ACRID VOLCANIC ROCK.

The drive back to Pahoa and Hilo via highway 132 is one of the prettiest in Hawai'i. Albrizzia trees, their trunks wrapped in thick green beards of philodendron, form a lacy canopy much of the way. Halfway to Pahoa, be sure to stop at Lava Trees State Monument, a lush little open-air terrarium. Everything is soaked in green. The attraction here is the lava molds formed around the trunks of an old 'ohi'a forest during an explosive eruption in the area in 1790.

New, uncooled *PAHOEHOE* LAVA GLISTENS WITH A SILVERY, PRISMATIC SHEEN LIKE THE SCALES OF FRESHLY CAUGHT FISH. THIS TYPE OF LAVA IS RECOGNIZED BY THE TWISTED, ROPY, BILLOWY, OR DRAPERY-LIKE PATTERNS THAT DEVELOP ON THE CRUST DURING THE FINAL MOMENTS OF CONGEALING. AS IT TRAVELS DOWNHILL, *PAHOEHOE* COMMONLY CHANGES TO 'A'A, THE ROUGH, JAGGED FRAGMENTS OF CRUST WHICH GEOLOGISTS ALSO CALL "CLINKER."

IF PELE BATHES IN THE SEA ON THE COAST OF PUNA, THE OCEAN BOILS, CREATING A WONDROUS, INDESCRIBABLE SCENE AS MOLTEN LAVA, SURGING SEA, AND EXPLOSIVE COLORS AND SOUNDS COALESCE IN ONE OF NATURE'S RAREST DISPLAYS OF VIOLENT SPLENDOR.

THE BLACK SANDS AT PUNALU'U BEACH NEAR SOUTH
POINT GET PRETTY HOT DURING MIDDAY HOURS, MAKING
A CASUAL WALK TO THE COOL, BLUE WATER NEARLY
IMPOSSIBLE WITHOUT SHOES.

KA'U

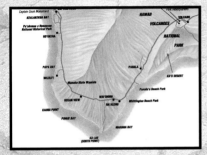

KALALEA, A WELL-PRESERVED FISHING SHRINE AT THE
SOUTHERNMOST TIP OF THE ISLAND, WAS *KAPU* (TABOO) TO
WOMEN. THROUGHOUT THE HISTORY OF THE REGION, MEN
HAVE LEFT OFFERINGS UPON THE ALTARS OF THIS
WALLED TEMPLE.

❋   ❋   ❋

Ka'u district (pronounced "Kah-OO"), including all of the Big Island's remote southern extremity, is Hawai'i's last frontier. Huge, "underpopulated," and "under-valued" according to some, Ka'u has been proposed as the site for a commercial rocket-launching facility. Ka'u residents resist the idea. Others see Ka'u as perfect for new destination resorts, including one called the "Hawaiian Riviera" and another on Ka'u's best beach at Punalu'u.

For others, Ka'u is a last stand, a fishing and agricultural community that does just fine without developers. For them the challenge is to preserve Ka'u's rural way of life. "Kapu Ka'u" says a common bumper sticker; it means "Ka'u is off-limits" or, less hospitably, "Keep out of Ka'u."

Little in Ka'u is designed to attract visitors. Its chief points of interest are geographically and historically significant Ka Lae (South Point), the towns of Wai'ohino and Na'alehu, and a lovely black-sand beach at Punalu'u. Most archaeologists and anthropologists agree that the Polynesians' first settlements in the Hawaiian archipelago were at or near the Big Island's southernmost tip. South Point's remains, carefully studied archaeologically, including Kalalea Heiau, numerous carved salt pans, a water hole, and the Makalei caves, are collectively known as the South Point Complex.

South Point is at the end of clearly marked, twelve-mile South Point Road, outside Na'alehu, at Highway 11's southernmost reach. The scenic drive dead-ends at the Kalahea Heiau, where the views back to Mauna Loa and up the western coast are put in perspective by the vast Pacific Ocean spreading to the southern, eastern, and western horizons. This is the southernmost point in the United States.

Ocean currents and deep water create ideal fishing just offshore. Wind and those same currents make the area hazardous for small boats, but fishermen have been working these waters since ancient times. Carved holes in the rocks just below the navigational marker were used by the Hawaiians to tether their canoes. Thus secured, the fishermen could cast their lures a few hundred feet offshore without worrying about the winds and currents that could easily drag them to sea.

✵   ✵   ✵   ✵

THE RUGGED COASTLINE OF KA'U IS THOUGHT TO HAVE BEEN THE FIRST LANDFALL MADE BY ANCIENT POLYNESIAN VOYAGERS. EXTENSIVE ARCHAEOLOGICAL EXCAVATIONS IN KA LAE MAKE IT ONE OF THE MOST SIGNIFICANT AREAS ON THE ISLAND TO EXAMINE THE EARLY CIVILIZATIONS OF HAWAI'I.

Three miles up the coast is an inaccessible and abandoned fishing village called Wai'ahukini, where scientists studying cave shelters have gathered the most conclusive proof yet that Hawai'i's earliest settlers were voyagers from the Marquesan Islands, 2,400 miles to the south, who arrived at least 1,400 years ago. The bone fish hooks found in the caves confirm Hawaiians' own legends of their long ocean voyages. The beach marking the ancient village is clearly visible up the west coast from South Point, just beyond the low cliffs.

ITINERANT CONGREGATIONAL MISSIONARIES PASSING THROUGH THE SOUTHERN DISTRICT OF KA'U WERE THE FIRST TO BRING CHRISTIANITY TO THE AREA. THEY GATHERED SMALL GROUPS OF HAWAIIANS TOGETHER AND PREACHED THE GOSPEL OF ONE GOD AND HIS SON, JESUS CHRIST. IN 1841 THEY ESTABLISHED THE KAUAOHA'AO CHURCH IN WAI'OHINU AND SUCCESSFULLY REPLACED THE DEFUNCT *KAPU* RELIGIOUS PRACTICES.

THESE SPINNING PROPELLERS AT SOUTH POINT ARE DRIVEN BY THE CEASELESS GUSTS THAT HAVE SHEARED THIS CAPE FOR EONS.

THE JAGGED SHORELINE OF PUNALU'U BEACH CREATES INTERESTING CONDITIONS FOR THE TRADITIONAL SUNBATHER. BOULDERS OF YOUNG LAVA CRACK AND TUMBLE INTO THE JOSTLING CURRENTS THAT ENDLESSLY WORK TO ERODE AND TAME PELE'S HANDIWORK ALONG THE KA'U COAST.

POHAKU KI'I (PETROGLYPHS) ARE CARVINGS SCRATCHED AND CHIPPED ON THE SURFACES OF STONES. BOULDERS, CLIFF FACES, AND RESTING PLACES ALONG LAVA FIELD TRAILS WERE COMMON CANVASES FOR CARVING.

THE OLIVINE COAST OF GREEN SAND BEACH, THREE MILES EAST OF SOUTH POINT, WAS CREATED BY THE COLLAPSE OF A SMALL CINDER CONE. THE BLACK LAVA GRAVEL SAND IS DOTTED WITH BUCKSHOT-SIZED GREEN CRYSTAL FRAGMENTS OF OLIVINE. SWIMMING HERE IS RELATIVELY SAFE ON CALM DAYS, BUT WHEN THE WINDS KICK UP THE SWELL AND HOWL THE SONGS OF LOST MARINERS, THE RAW POWER OF OPEN-OCEAN WAVES BATTERS THIS LITTLE INLET.

THE WOOD VALLEY TEMPLE IN THE PUNA DISTRICT IS A STANDING TESTAMENT TO THE ORIENTAL IMMIGRANTS BROUGHT IN TO HARVEST THE VAST FIELDS OF SUGAR CANE. SET AGAINST A BACKDROP OF ʻOHIʻA, THIS COMPLEX OF BUILDING HAS SERVED THE AREA AS A CENTER OF WORSHIP FOR OVER 50 YEARS.

LOCAL FISHERMEN AND THEIR FAMILIES FREQUENT THIS "MOM AND POP" FRUIT STAND ON THE SLEEPY DOWNTOWN STREETS OF NAʻALEHU. LITERALLY TRANSLATED, THE HAWAIIAN NAME OF THIS SMALL KAʻU COMMUNITY MEANS "VOLCANIC ASHES," AN APT DESCRIPTION OF THE TREMENDOUS AMOUNTS OF LAVA IN THE REGION.

THE SOUTHERN CAPE OF THE BIG ISLAND IS KNOWN AS SOUTH POINT. MANY STILL USE ITS OLD HAWAIIAN NAME, KA LAE, "THE POINT."

THE BEACH FRONTING THE MAUNA LANI
BAY HOTEL AND BUNGALOWS INVITES THE
WEARY TO RELAX IN A PEACEFUL SETTING
OF DECADENT PAMPERING. LEEWARD
WEATHER, BALMY BREEZES, AND THE
CONSTANT LAPPING OF GENTLE WAVES ON A
SHORE OF WHITE SAND MAKE THIS THE
IDEAL MILIEU FOR UNWINDING.

BEACHES

THE BIG ISLAND IS TOO young for either big beaches, barrier reefs, or much coral sand to have formed. Many of its most popular beach spots make do with gray, salt-and-pepper, or black sand, where lava is the source. There are even a few green-sand beaches, colored so by olivine crystals. Some terrific swimming areas have no sand at all.

The biggest Big Island beach news of the past decade has been the loss of two of its most scenic strands. The twin black-sand beaches at historic Kalapana and Kaimu in Puna, with their lovely coconut groves and deep blue waters, were obliterated in 1990 by lava flows.

The Big Island still has more than 100 beaches along its 300-plus-mile coastline. Some are stunningly beautiful, the kind you see in travel posters. While there are often no lifeguards on duty, most of the twenty established beach parks and recreation areas have restrooms, showers, and parking.

The following menu of the Big Island's best beaches is designed to help you choose your perfect beach day. And by all means spend at least one complete day at a beach, preferably one facing west to the sunset. Watching the new or full moon after a glorious Hawaiian sunset is the ultimate experience with Hawai'i's overwhelming natural beauty.

NOTE: All beaches in Hawai'i are public property up to the vegetation line above the high-water mark. Whenever waterfront development occurs, particularly for beachfront resorts and residential communities, public access to the shore must be provided. In these areas, beach rights-of-way from public roads are marked—some better than others.

Kauna'oa (Mauna Kea) Beach

LAURENCE ROCKEFELLER KNEW WHAT HE WAS DOING
WHEN HE LEASED KAUNA'OA BEACH FROM THE PARKER
RANCH TO BUILD A LUXURY HOTEL IN 1965. THE
SUPREMELY ISOLATED, UNDERSTATED MAUNA KEA
BEACH HOTEL, COMMANDING THE MOST BEAUTIFUL
BEACH ON THE ENTIRE ISLAND QUICKLY CLAIMED
DISTINCTION AMONG THE EXCLUSIVE AND CELEBRATED
RESORT HOTELS OF THE WORLD. KAUNA'OA IS A PERFECT
CRESCENT OF WHITE SAND, FRINGED WITH PALMS AND
NAUPAKA AND SET BETWEEN TWO LAVA POINTS. THE
SANDY BOTTOM SLOPES GENTLY INTO THE OPEN OCEAN.
WAVE ACTION IS CALM IN SUMMER, ALTHOUGH THE
WINTER SHORE BREAK CAN BE VIOLENT. GENERALLY, THE
BEACH PROVIDES EXCELLENT SWIMMING AND
SNORKELING, EXCEPT DURING HEAVY SURF.

'Anaeho'omalu Bay

PALM-FRINGED 'ANAEHO'OMALU BAY LIES AT THE EDGE OF
MAUNA KEA'S SWEEPING WESTERN FLANK ON THE DRY, LAVA-
STREWN SOUTH KOHALA COAST. THIS SPECTACULAR BAY HAS
THE FEELING OF AN OPEN STAGE INSIDE A GREAT AMPITHEATER.
ALL AROUND IT, BROAD SLOPES CLIMB TO THE CLOUD-CLOAKED
HEIGHTS OF KOHALA, MAUNA KEA, MAUNA LOA, AND
HUALĀLAI. ACROSS THE SEA, LOOKING IMPOSSIBLY LOFTY ON
THE NORTHWESTERN HORIZON, IS THE PEAK OF MAUI'S 10,000-
FOOT HALEAKALĀ, ABOUT 80 MILES AWAY.

Hapuna Beach

THIS IS THE BIG ISLAND'S FAVORITE BEACH AND ONE OF ITS BIGGEST. A HALF-MILE LONG AND 200 FEET WIDE IN SUMMER, HAPUNA HANDLES THE BIG CROWDS, ESPECIALLY ON WEEKENDS, WHEN RESIDENTS FROM AS FAR AWAY AS HILO AND PUNA FLOCK TO THIS SUNNY SHORE AND ITS LIMPID WATERS. THE BEACH IS A WIDE CRESCENT LIKE KAUNA'OA, ITS NEIGHBOR TO THE NORTH, ONLY LARGER AND BISECTED BY A ROCK OUTCROPPING. THE LAND BEHIND THE NORTH END OF THE BEACH IS PRIVATELY OWNED AND MAY SOON BE THE SITE OF A RESORT HOTEL. THE BACKSHORE TO THE SOUTH IS LANDSCAPED BEACH PARK LAND WITH SHOWERS, RESTROOMS, A PAVILLION, A FEW CABINS AVAILABLE FOR RENT, AND A LARGE PARKING LOT.

Kehena

KEHENA BEACH IS ONE OF HAWAI'I'S MOST SCENIC
AND LEAST-KNOWN CLOTHING OPTIONAL SUNBATHING
BEACHES. SITTING AT THE BASE OF 50-FOOT SEA CLIFFS,
ABOUT THREE MILES NORTH OF NOW-DESTROYED
KALAPANA, KEHENA WAS FORMED IN 1955 BY LAVA
SPILLING INTO THE SEA NEARBY. IT WAS ALTERED AGAIN
BY AN EARTHQUAKE IN 1975, WHICH CAUSED THE
BEACH TO SUBSIDE ABOUT THREE FEET. FOR THE
MOMENT , AT LEAST, THE LOVELY BEACH IS DIVIDED INTO
TWO COVES BY A ROCKY RIDGE THAT ACCOMMODATES
THE STEEP TRAIL FROM THE HIGHWAY. THE COVE TO THE
RIGHT IS OFTEN SWEPT CLEAN BY WAVE ACTION AND IS
NOT USED. THE LARGER COVE TO THE LEFT IS QUITE
WIDE, WITH COCONUTS, *KAMANI*, AND IRONWOODS
FORMING A SHADY BACKSHORE UNDER THE CLIFFS.

Leleiwi Beach Park

One of Hilo's most scenic and least "touristy" spots, this waterfront park has something for almost everyone. Set along a bit of rocky coast east of Hilo's port area, the park is a long series of inlets, coves, tidal pools, a few black-sand pockets, and a bay protected by a string of rocky islands at the eastern end. Classic views across Hilo Bay to Mauna Kea and the Hamakua coast form an idyllic background.

THE FANTASY OF HORSEBACK RIDING ALONG
WAIPI'O'S ISOLATED BLACK-SAND BEACH,
FLANKED BY SHEER VALLEY CLIFFS, LUSH RAIN
FORESTS, AND THE TEAL BLUE OF DEEP OCEAN,
IS JUST A PHONE CALL AWAY.

ADVENTURES

HIGH-ENERGY WIND AND sea conditions and year-round warmth make the Big Island—like the rest of Hawai'i—an athletic natural. The islands have become a great watersports capital. International athletes flock to its surf contests, long-distance swimming races, offshore deep-sea fishing tournaments, canoe and kayak races, windsurfing contests, and inter-island and trans-Pacific yacht races. On shore, brawny triathletes, daring hang gliders, and mud-stained hikers and bicyclists carry the "just do it" ethos to new extremes.

Energy is everywhere on the Big Island—in the big mid-Pacific water, in the stiff trade winds, and on this young volcanic island itself. You can feel the vibrant energy as soon as you arrive.

Horseback Riding

More than any of the other islands, Hawai'i is ranch country. British Navy Captain George Vancouver put ashore a few head of cattle in 1790 as gifts for the young chief Kamehameha. Taking care of those cattle became the responsibility of John Parker, who founded Parker Ranch, a spread of 225,000 acres in South Kohala. The Parker Ranch, Kahua Ranch, Pu'uwa'awa'a Ranch, Greenwell Ranch, Hualālai

A SMALL FLEET OF RECREATIONAL CHARTERS OUT OF KAILUA-KONA TOWN OFFERS SNORKELING AND SCUBA TOURS TO BEACHES THAT ARE INACCESSIBLE BY LAND. ARMED WITH MASKS, SNORKELS, BOOGIE-BOARDS, AND FINS, THESE INTREPID YOUNGSTERS BRAVE THE PRISTINE UNDERWATER WORLD OF THE YOUNGEST ISLAND IN THE PACIFIC.

Ranch, and several others, all carry on as cattle ranches. It's the land of *paniolos*, those Hawaiian cowboys who somehow manage to put an essentially Hawaiian twist on the best of the old West.

Trail rides are popular on the island's vast grasslands, from the impossibly green hills of Kamuela and Kohala to the silvery high deserts of Waikoloa. Kahua Ranch offers horseback access to its glorious Kohala highlands, with daily morning rides, as well as customized outings and adventures. Cross-country rides are also available through the windswept Montana-like pasture lands of Waikoloa.

For something different, splash through Waipi'o Valley's streams and along its black-sand beach on horseback.

Deep Sea Fishing

Whether you're an experienced big game fisherman or a fly-fishing aficionado eager to see what a big one feels like, you should not pass up the rich sport fishing on the Kona coast. The deep water close to shore draws black, Pacific blue and striped marlin; yellowfin tuna ('*ahi*); dolphin fish

A VISIT TO THE ANTHURIUM FARMS AND BOTANICAL GARDENS ON THE BIG ISLAND IS A REWARDING EXPERIENCE FOR FLOWER LOVERS OF ALL AGES. THESE HEART-SHAPED BLOSSOMS ARE SOMETIMES CALLED "LITTLE BOY FLOWERS," AND CAN BE PURCHASED FROM OPEN-MARKET VENDORS OR ORDERED TO BE SENT ANYWHERE IN THE WORLD.

✳   ✳   ✳

(*mahimahi*); wahoo (*ono*); sailfish; spearfish; amberjacks; and mako sharks. An hour or two spent wrestling a Pacific Blue, and then finding that the beast weighs over 300 pounds is a once-in-a-lifetime thrill. (Try not to think about how much you'll be paying the taxidermist.)

The old pier at Kailua-Kona was fishing headquarters until the U.S. Army Corps of Engineers dredged nearby Honokohau Harbor in 1980. The bustling artificial harbor is now home port for a very competitive ninety-boat charter fleet eager to help you catch the big one.

Rates vary considerably, ranging from excursions per person for half-day shared boats, up to exclusive private all-day charters with as many as six passengers. Full-day charters sometimes include food. To arrange a charter, contact one of the booking agencies or head down to the harbor in the late afternoon, eyeball the boats, talk to the skippers, and make your own arrangements.

The seasonal *Kona Fishing and Travel Guide*, published by the Hawai'i Visitors Bureau, is available at most hotel travel desks.

ALL IT TAKES IS A BACK-PACKED LUNCH, A RENTED BIKE, AND A SOLID HELMET FOR A RIDE DOWN THE MOUNTAINS OF THE BIG ISLAND.

STUNNING, PREHISTORIC-LOOKING RED JADE VINES HANG IN CASCADING CRIMSON AT THE ELEGANT NANI MAU BOTANICAL GARDENS JUST OUTSIDE OF HILO. THIS BEAUTIFUL PARK HAS ONE OF THE LARGEST COLLECTIONS OF ORCHIDS IN HAWAI'I, AND IS FAMOUS FOR ITS RARE AND EXOTIC FLOWERS.

A Walk in the Garden

Scientists estimate that about four hundred species of plants gained a footing in Hawai'i in the ten million years between its fiery creation and the arrival of the first Polynesians. These plants arrived at a rate of one species every 20,000 years, evolving into about 2,200 native plants, many of which are now extinct.

THE CLASSIC CATTLEYA ORCHID AND ITS MANY RELATIVES CAN BE SEEN IN THE BIG ISLAND'S NURSERIES AND FORMAL GARDENS.

✳   ✳   ✳

The Polynesians brought with them the plants they needed to survive. Among them were coconut palms, *ti*, bananas, *taro*, *kukui*, mulberry, sugar cane, and a few more. Westerners introduced crop plants and ornamentals, some of which are today's weeds. Many of Hawai'i's characteristic plants—pineapples, most orchids, anthuriums, fragrant plumeria—are not native. But they all flourish in the Islands' well-watered volcanic soil.

The Puna and Hamakua districts of the Big Island are Hawai'i's flower-growing centers. Hilo's commercial nurseries produce fabulous cattleya orchids for export, as well as shiny red anthuriums, and spectacular heliconias. There are several orchid nurseries to visit in the Hilo area and up the Volcano Road beyond Glenwood. Ask the locals for recommendations and directions.

Well known for its orchid collection, the heavily-manicured **Nani Mau Garden** is outside Hilo on Volcano Road. Once inside the gates, visitors can rent golf carts or ride the tram to view the grounds. Particularly interesting are the jade vines, both the traditional green and a blazing orange variety.

The **Hawaii Tropical Botanical Garden**, another paid attraction, is five miles north of Hilo. Its overall feeling is more in keeping with the tropical ideal of riotous greenery edged by the blue Pacific.

At nearby **Akaka Falls State Park**, the path to the falls passes through a beautiful, mature garden, planted in the 1920s. In addition to being free, these gardens represent artful naturalism.

Kalopa State Recreation Area, off the Hawai'i Belt Road (Highway 19) above the town of Honoka'a, is a little-known forest reserve laced with well-kept trails. The forest features native 'ohi'a groves, as well as towering stands of eucalyptus, ironwood, and tropical ash. The fragrant air is cool and moist and sometimes even wet—typical of Mauna Kea's upland windward weather. The access road is marked by signs off the main highway just east of Honoka'a town.

The ultimate in Japanese restraint and serenity is **Lili'uokalani Gardens** overlooking Hilo Bay, just off Banyan Drive, with a restful design and peaceful views across Hilo Bay.

THE SACRED PRECINCTS OF PU'UHONUA O HONAUNAU NATIONAL HISTORICAL PARK OFFER A FASCINATING GLIMPSE INTO ANCIENT HAWAI'I. THERE IS ALSO EXCELLENT SNORKELING TO BE ENJOYED NEARBY.

Snorkeling

Anywhere on the Big Island's west coast where there is sand, calm water, and a rocky point, you'll find beautiful snorkeling. Prime spots include the little cove at Lapakahi State Park and Mahukona Harbor in North Kohala; Spencer, Kauna'oa, Hapuna, Puako, Mauna Lani, and 'Anaeho'omalu beaches in South Kohala, and Kahalu'u, Keauhou, Kealakekua, and Honaunau in the Kona district (see Beaches). Near Hilo, the protected cove at Richardson Ocean Center in Leleiwi Beach Park is a favorite snorkeling spot.

SNORKELING IS A WONDERFUL ADVENTURE FOR KIDS, AND A CHANCE TO GET CLOSE TO AN UNDERWATER WORLD OF MAGIC.

✻   ✻   ✻

Of all these sites, Kealakekua Bay stands out. This scenic and historic bay has an unusual abundance of dramatic corals and fish and its waters are a marine conservation zone. Commercial tour boats visit the bay on most days. Your hotel activities desk can provide more information about the many seaborne snorkeling tours from Kailua-Kona and Keauhou.

Honaunau Bay, four miles south of Kealakekua, has marvelous, uncrowded snorkeling guarded by the ancient for-tifications of **Pu'uhonua o Honaunau National Historical Park**. Park rules discourage swimmers from entering the water from the sacred compound, but there are good entry points at the boat ramp on Honaunau Bay, or overlooking Alahaka Bay.

Extreme caution is needed when swimming anywhere on the island, particularly during winter. Swim fins are always a good idea.

One last suggestion for wintertime snorkelers and divers: when you're in open water, take a moment to sink a few feet beneath the surface facing the open ocean. Be perfectly still as long as you can, and listen. With any luck, you'll hear the faint clicks, creaky moans, and high-pitched squeals of the humpback whales who are in the water with you, enjoying their winter in Hawai'i.

Hiking

The most unusual hiking trips on the Big Island are into Kīlauea's volcanic landscapes. **Hawai'i Volcanoes National Park** has a network of trails, as well as a sensitive treatment of archaeological and geological sites.

Some suggested hikes in and around Kīlauea: Probe six miles into the fabled Ka'u Desert via the **Mauna Iki Trail**, between Hawai'i Belt Road and Hilina Pali Road, to see the petrified, 200-year-old footprints in the ash of a Hawaiian army surprised by a sudden explosive eruption; or take the **Halape Trail** from the highlands to the sea, to

GUIDED TOURS WITH EXPERIENCED NAUI INSTRUCTORS TAKE VISITORS ON SCUBA-DIVING EXCURSIONS DOWN THE ROCKY, UNDERWATER SLOPES OF THE TALLEST MOUNTAIN IN THE WORLD.

GUIDED TOURS THROUGH THE LUSH RAIN FORESTS THAT DRAPE THE WINDWARD SLOPES OF MAUNA LOA ARE PROVIDED BY THE NATIONAL PARK SERVICE. SHOULD YOU PLAN TO EXPLORE THE TERRAIN ON YOUR OWN, THE VOLCANOES NATIONAL PARK VISITOR CENTER CAN PROVIDE USEFUL MAPS TO HELP YOU ON YOUR ADVENTURE THROUGH THE NETWORK OF CLEARLY MARKED TRAILS TO ARCHAEOLOGICAL AND GEOLOGICAL SITES.

the remains of a submerged coconut grove, a cove beach, and the shelter at Halape. It's a fifteen-mile round trip, best done with an overnight stay at the beachside shelter.

Simpler, shorter hikes include the half-mile **Devastation Trail**, the dramatic three-mile loop of the **Kīlauea Iki Trail**, the .8 mile **Napau Crater Trail** to Pu'u Huluhulu and the Mauna Ulu over-look, and the one-mile walk to the petroglyphs at Pu'u Loa via the **Pu'u Loa Trail** off the lower Chain of Craters Road. Before doing any hiking in the park, check at the Visitor Center. Overnight hikers *must* register with Park officials before heading out.

SUBFREEZING TEMPERATURES AT THE SUMMIT OF MAUNA KEA ("WHITE MOUNTAIN") FREQUENTLY DRAPE THE VOLCANO IN SNOW. SKIERS TAKE FOUR-WHEEL DRIVE VEHICLES TO THE SUMMIT TO ENJOY THE THRILL OF ITS SLEEP SLOPES. THE RIDE IS A BUMPY ONE, BOTH ON WHEELS AND ON SKIS. THE ROADS ARE UNIMPROVED AND THE SKI RUNS ARE LITTERED WITH ROCKS AND CRUSTED ICE.

✳   ✳   ✳

The North Kohala coast offers an easy hike into **Pololu Valley** via the trail head at Pololu lookout, at the end of Highway 270.

At the opposite end of the same coast, a twenty-minute, very steep downhill walk leads into **Waipi'o Valley**, the legendary Valley of the Kings, and an excellent spot for overnight camping and exploring.

Or, better yet, make reservations at the smallest, most basic hotel on the island and the only hotel in Waipi'o— **Tom's Inn**, aka **Tom Araki's place**, aka the **Waipi'o Hotel**. By whichever name, there's no electricity, no food, and no hot showers, so it's just like camping out. The bonuses include clean bed linens, the novelty of spending around $20 per night, and excellent company. As night falls, the kerosene lanterns are lit and peace descends upon the deep valley. The stories and contentment often continue until past midnight. Reserve ahead; this place is popular.

Snow Skiing

Yes, there is usually snow each winter on the top 1,000 or 2,000 feet of Mauna Kea and Mauna Loa. And yes, sometimes, when temperature and wind conditions are right, it's skiable. But it's rare for wind, snow, air temperature, sunlight, and skiers to meet in perfect harmony. And even when they do, you still have to contend with "lite" air that has 40 percent less oxygen in it. Still, if you want to say you've done it, give it a try.

Trips to Mauna Kea's summit are provided by a local shuttle company with four-wheel-drive vehicles. Again, inquire locally or at your hotel front desk. However you go, you must provide your own ski equipment.